Finding Joy in
Leadership

By Developing Trust You Can Count On

Dr Ray R. Phillips

For information, contact
BDI Publishers, Atlanta, Georgia,
bdipublishers@gmail.com.

Cover Design: Vanessa Mendozzi
Layout Design: Tudor Maier
BDI Publishers

Atlanta, Georgia
ISBN: 978-1-946637-27-7
FIRST EDITION

I dedicate this book to all the amazing leaders I was privileged to work with during my Air Force career, and who modeled and inspired me to take care of those whom I, in turn, was privileged to lead.

Contents

Acknowledgments

There is nothing like a synergistic organization for leaders and followers where selfless mutual support and commitment provide a force multiplier like no other. When one has tasted synergy, you long for it in every organization you are a part of. This book has been a work in progress for over four decades, beginning with my high school basketball team and continuing to this day—from Mr Frank Javernick, who gave me my first real chance at leadership, to the exceptional leaders I was fortunate to work with during my 23 years of military service.

I am a product of each of these leaders who took the time to invest in the future and make our world a better place in which to live. Because of them, I have tasted synergy, and my passion for this book was to illustrate the process it takes to "find joy in leadership" and so experience that synergistic feeling. Another great man and basketball coach, Mr Bob Miles, taught me early in my life (fourth grade) that life—and our team, for that matter—was not about *me*!

Nothing I have accomplished in my life has been done on my own. Every success has been due to the selfless support of those who have helped me on my journey. This book is no exception. Without the support of a special group of people who stood by, encouraged, and counseled me, this book would never have happened.

First and foremost, I would like to recognize my "band of brothers" who have been with me from reviewing my Ph.D. dissertation and through every part of this book. Rear Admiral (Retired) Dick Brooks, who truly epitomizes leading by example and a positive attitude toward problem-solving, encouraged the creativity and approach to making this book applicable to the leader and student of leadership alike. To this day, Dick remains committed to developing leaders of the future.

Dr Mike Spencer is an inspiration to anyone who has the privilege of working with him. A soldier's soldier, Mike epitomizes personal and professional growth. His common sense approach to just about any subject cuts through the verbiage and focuses on the points to be made. If you enjoy the direct nature of the process in this book, it is Mike to be thanked!

Colonel (Retired) Bob Reehoorn is nothing short of an amazing communicator! Bob's tireless time devoted to reviewing drafts transformed this manuscript from a collection of stories and theories to a compelling read that I hope will inspire leaders for decades to come. Transparent communications are Bob's trademark!

Dr Colonel (Retired) Ron Scott has guided, mentored, and inspired me from the day I thought about pursuing a Ph.D. through my dissertation defense to the completion of this book. Ron is an unapologetic pathfinder and critical thinker, tirelessly committed to advancing the leadership cause toward making our world and nation better places!

In addition to this band of brothers, there are countless leaders and followers who have shaped me and my study of this curious relationship that we call "leadership". In addition, there were several acquaintances I was fortunate enough to meet on the golf course or be seated next to in the airplane who offered perspectives on leadership.

I'm grateful to my editor, Anne Abel Smith, whose patience and proficient skills have given this book life and energy beyond my expectations. And, finally, a very special thanks and appreciation to my partner in life who is (and has always been) there for me when I needed inspiration and encouragement. My wonderful wife and family are the ones who help me keep my character and reputation congruent and in check. I am so appreciative of all of you for your support in *Finding Joy in Leadership*.

Introduction:
Reward or Joy?

E very year, thousands of articles on leadership are written in various scholarly journals. According to a survey in 2013, there were over 15,000 leadership books in print at that time.[1] In a 2015 article on leadership books, Cairnway, an executive coaching firm, claimed that Amazon offered 57,136 books with the word "leadership" in the title![2] So, why another book on leadership? Or, perhaps more personally, what will you get out of reading this book? What is in it for you? The answer to these questions lies in the distinction between reward and joy.

Leadership has been debated since the early days of the Chinese strategist Sun Tzu, who wrote his famous book, *The Art of War*, between 475 and 221 BC. Those who assumed leadership roles soon became scholarly research subjects in the never-ending quest to understand those who chose to lead. The question of whether leaders were born or made was quickly followed by leadership theories that sought to address this same question to explain various approaches to this curious relationship. No different from psychology's quest to explain human

---

1 Shinagel, M. (2013, July 3). The Paradox of Leadership. Harvard Extension School, Professional Development Blog. https://blog.dce.harvard.edu/professional-development/paradox-leadership
2 Iarocci, J. (2015, October 26). Why are there so many leadership books? Here are 5 reasons. https://serveleadnow.com/why-are-there-so-many-leadership-books

behavior, the dynamics of explaining leadership also take into account human behavior and human response.

As biological creatures, our bodies respond to different stimuli by releasing chemical hormones in the brain. When we achieve a high grade on a test, are selected for advancement or promotion, or receive a bonus, our brains respond by releasing dopamine and we relish in the motivational salience of the reward. Unfortunately, the dopamine feeling diminishes soon after the reward has been received and we are left wanting more. Biologically, the subsequent desire—or craving—is often greater than the original boost!

On the other hand, when we find joy in what we do, our behavior is a reward in itself. Our brains release serotonin as well as dopamine, and both provide long-term satisfaction contributing to well-being and happiness. This true sense of satisfaction is constantly reinforced as we continue doing what we find joy in doing. When leaders find joy in the leadership process, their well-being and happiness inspire those they lead and create a bond of trust, further strengthening the leadership relationship.

As we experience the strengthening of such a relationship, our body releases another powerful hormone called 'oxytocin', which supports social recognition, trust, and respect. This is the same hormone that is released when a mother nurses her newborn child, thereby creating that special bond of trust between the two. In the workplace, these bonds of trust and respect serve as catalysts for success and enjoyment. Finding joy in leadership is a critical element for an organization and the individuals within it when trust and respect are present.

Seeking to understand the difference between reward and joy will be beneficial to a broad audience— from a college student or mid-level manager to a senior executive. I hope everyone in the leadership arena will find it both interesting and enlightening, by providing the aspiring leader with:

- a proven approach to building trust in leadership relationships;

- a common-sense approach to effective leadership;

- a formula for relishing the leadership experience and so making the workplace enjoyable for both leaders and followers;

- a procedure for bridging the gap between the MBA curriculum and practical leadership;

- a "predictability" within the leadership relationship to reduce the stress of speculation and expectation;

- a positive "team" atmosphere whereby all team members know *why* they are there and *how* their actions support that purpose; and

- a process that can be applied to any leadership theory and style.

This is not another leadership theory book. Rather, it is written for current and future leaders, offering an approach for them and their organizations to thrive and experience real joy in the process. Having spent over four decades studying leadership (the theory, if you will) and filling leadership positions (the practice), I have found joy in leadership and have honed personal perspectives on what works to achieve this remarkable level of satisfaction.

My passion is for leaders to find joy in leadership and for organizations to thrive under this type of leadership. When the leader knows *why* they chose to lead, understands the *potential challenges* ahead, acknowledges that *joy must be pursued*, knows the importance of *establishing a culture* for success, and has a *proven process* for creating that culture, they have the *ingredients to find joy in leadership*. This book provides all the components needed to **Find Joy in Leadership by Developing Trust You Can Count On**.

As a final note, I have aimed to address leadership across the spectrum, from students to senior executives. To that end, I have posed questions to consider and a "Takeaway" from each section. The questions are intended for both individual and group discussions, and might be insightful for both leader and follower to contemplate together. It may also be helpful to examine the class curriculum's theoretical approach to leadership with the questions' practical perspective within the classroom.

Finally, each successive part of this book builds on the last. My goal is to generate thoughts and questions as you read through each part, and then to address those questions as you read further. As with any process, mastering the fundamentals will come with time and application but—with perseverance—comes the transition from good to great. Have fun, persevere, and discover the path to finding joy in leadership!

Part I:

Why People Seek Leadership Positions

From that first time on the playground when the teacher selected two captains to choose dodgeball teams, it became clear that being a leader had advantages. Our perceptions were awakened to this selection process and we had to consider these opportunities. Whether being chosen to lead the Pledge of Allegiance, to be the first chair in the band, class leader, or captain of the sports team, it became natural to relate leadership selection as a special honor or reward even though additional responsibilities were attached to the position. Despite these added responsibilities, the joy of being selected seemed to outweigh those expectations.

Those early days were reinforced throughout the educational process as honor societies, class officers, and athletic scholarships identified those leading the way. The reward for being a recognized leader continued to resonate through most of these formative years, although the responsibilities and demands seemed to become more significant. Ask any college athlete about their sport's demands throughout the year, and they will tell you they never really stop: one must truly love the sport, or find joy in it, to stay engaged.

Ah, the light comes on, and we reflect on the well-known saying, "To whom much is given, much will be required"[3]. If you compete at the highest levels of any endeavor, you must genuinely love what you do and be committed to your team and its shared goals. However, when we examine organizations rather than sports, we find many leaders advancing through the ranks whose passion and commitment are not always prerequisites for selection.

In most cases, within organizations, prerequisites are previous experience, advanced education, and a demonstrated potential to help the organization succeed. And let's be completely honest: at times, the "who you know" comes into play. It can be challenging to determine love and commitment to an organization in the interview process. In reality, this is a "wait and see" activity, most often assumed and quickly forgotten. It is common for leaders to be hired solely on their abilities as experts in their fields. A central assumption is that they can lead others to do the same.

The promotion system often assumes that top performers will make excellent leaders but—unfortunately—that is often not the case. Having worked in the information technology (IT) industry for nearly a decade, I can attest that some of the greatest IT specialists are not the least interested in either leadership or management. In the aviation industry, some of the finest pilots and mechanics are happy just where they are,

---

3 Bible, New International Version, 2016, (Luke 12:48).

and they too often view management or leadership as for those who cannot fly or turn a wrench. The point is that we need leaders who know *why* they are leading, and who want to find joy in that leadership.

What does a leadership position mean to people?

- For some, accepting a leadership position is about the prestige of the role. We need only reflect on our first high school reunion, where the primary conversation topic was an inquiry about your job or position in life. Answering this question with a title connoting a leadership position feels good to many because we all appreciate some level of affirmation.

- Some people seek leadership positions for power and control so that they can call the shots and choose the team. To them, it feels good to be the boss.

- Then others wish to be a part of something greater than themselves and have a positive impact on the lives of those within their sphere of influence. They view leadership as a privilege and a gift not to be taken for granted.

This list is not meant to be all-inclusive: it is intended instead to illustrate different reasons why people accept leadership positions. Both the leader and the organization must know why they have chosen to lead and that they are committed to that cause. The following examples illustrate real-world stories of different leadership situations and the *why* behind the decision-making. They highlight a time *to* change, a time *for* change, and a time *of* change. As you read through each of these examples, consider your own leadership experiences and ask yourself the following questions:

- Have I experienced this type of leadership?

- Was it effective?

- What impact did it have on the organization?

Example 1: A Time *to* Change—Re-focusing the "why"

The small business owner had scheduled a strategic planning meeting with the CEO to discuss the way ahead for the coming year. The meeting was scheduled for 9 a.m. in the company conference room, as was usual when the owner wanted to map out ideas for the following year using the whiteboards. He was visually oriented and this had been his standard approach in his seven years working with the CEO.

During those seven years, the organization had grown from 50 employees and $5 million in revenue to over 150 employees and $60 million in revenue. The catalyst for this growth was the organization's focus on integrity and taking care of its employees who, in their turn, took care of the customers. Their success brought with it multiple awards and recognition for the organization throughout the community and across the industry.

The owner entered the conference room, sat down facing the CEO with a somber look, and said it was time *to* change. He made it clear that he would now be the CEO to cut costs and increase margins. The CEO would be laid off and there would also be other layoffs within the company. While the company had seen tremendous growth and recognition in the past seven years, the owner wanted to shift the organization's focus from an integrity-first, people-focused culture to a leaner and more efficient structure—in order to increase margins and make some *real* money. Apparently, it was time *to* change from leading people (and the success that approach had achieved) to strictly managing the numbers.

Takeaway: There are many reasons people seek leadership positions, not the least of which is to explore their entrepreneurial spirit and make a difference in the world. In this story, the owner had started this small business with the vision of creating an integrity-focused services company leveraging his prior experience in business development for a large company to provide these services to the growing small business community. In the beginning, this was a reasonable and honorable endeavor.

The integrity-centered focus attracted not only those who would work for this company but also those who would solicit its services. As Simon Sinek suggests in his best-selling book, *Start with Why*,[4] this company's

4 Sinek, S. (2009). Start with why: How great leaders inspire everyone to take action. Penguin.

21

why was to provide IT services to the community by creating an integrity-focused culture of employees committed to that cause. Trust was fostered both within and throughout this organization.

This selfless vision, combined with a committed organizational culture, enabled the owner to realize his entrepreneurial spirit and make a difference in the community, and to do so consistently—*until* the focus shifted from people to numbers. Success often brings a leader to the crossroads of sharing their wealth with those who helped them succeed or deciding to cash in because, after all, this success is about them!

This company still exists today, but its growth has atrophied, the vision has been diluted, and the employees no longer feel a part of something greater than themselves. Instead, they are operating in survival mode, hoping they can retain their jobs.

Indeed, this small business went from thriving to surviving when the owner decided that it was time *to* change from focusing on people to managing numbers. While this may seem very short-sighted, it is a common approach in today's workplace. Leaders' aims are monetary gains, either for themselves or for their shareholders. Underlying this leadership approach is a focus on the short-term "dopamine" reward.

Although it may feel great to increase margins and make "real" money, this near-sighted focus becomes a yearly grind. Like NFL Super Bowl champions celebrating their victory until the next season starts, organizations focused on annual revenue targets and year-end bonuses must start the process all over again once their new fiscal year, or season, starts. Focusing on monetary rewards can only provide short-term success. However, our next example will show leading with a passion for the people in an organization can create lasting success.

Questions to consider:

- What is more critical: employees who support the company's profits or the profits that pay the employee?

- What is the difference between managing the numbers and leading the organization?

Example 2: A Time *for* Change—Leading with Passion for Your Employees

The aircraft hangar was pristine, set with chairs to accommodate over 2,000 attendees, and a sizable American flag served as a backdrop to an elevated stage. As in many military ceremonial settings, the aura was one of pride and expectation: pride for the organization's accomplishments and expectation for even greater successes in the future.

Members of the organization were present to witness the time *for* change from one leader to another, the honored military tradition of the Change of Command.

23

The focus of this change is on the organization and the people who make it successful. The past two years under the leadership of the outgoing leader had been anything but uneventful: there was the war in the Balkans, the bombing of the USS Cole, and the attacks on 9/11. In addition to these unforeseen events, there were multiple exercises, personnel issues, and organizational challenges. Each of these events, foreseen and unforeseen, created common bonds between members of the organization, strengthening their culture of excellence.

During his tenure, the current leader had established a theme, "Reflection of Excellence", whereby everyone knew they were playing a significant role in the nations defense and were charged to reflect daily on their contributions. There was no doubt *why* they were there or *why* the organization was essential. During each day's foreseen and unforeseen challenges, their *why* guided them to give their best, knowing they were a part of something greater than themselves.

The supervisor begins the ceremony by discussing the organization's accomplishments under the outgoing leader's leadership. The comments on his leadership are primarily addressed to the organization. The discussion centers around how far the organization has come during these times of adversity and how it rose to take on unforeseen challenges. It is essentially a "Reflection of Excellence" of this group's performance during the outgoing leader's tenure.

The comments then shift to the incoming leader and the potential they bring to advancing the organization's vision and mission. Equipped with a similar skill set and leadership style to those of the outgoing leader, the incoming leader's background is discussed in the context of the organization's mission and why it is anticipated that they will justify the leadership position. The theme for this time *for* change is more about what the incoming leader can do for the organization's advancement than what the organization can do to promote the leader. This focus is deliberate because this leadership position is not about managing numbers: it is about the passion required to lead and care for those one has the privilege of leading and who ultimately make the organization successful.

The outgoing leader then speaks to the group, acknowledging all that they have collectively accomplished during this time together, and encouraging them to continue achieving under the incoming leader. This leader recognizes the gift of potentially making an impact on those in the organization during their time of leadership. Each member of the organization knows their role, and each views leadership as the catalyst for realizing their potential to be their absolute best.

Finally, the incoming leader addresses the members of the organization, acknowledging its accomplishments and introducing a vision to advance each individual and the unit collective to reach higher in the quest for continued excellence. To make this vision a reality, the new leader must gain the organization's trust through their actions, just as the previous leader had done. This trust, such a dynamic element within a mutually accountable relationship, fosters even higher levels of excellence.

Takeaway: This time *for* change differs from the previous time *to* change with the critical aspect of focusing on the people, not the numbers. With this example, we see clearly that leadership is not about profits, power, or prestige but about the people. To be clear, selecting the right leader must seek to find someone with a passion for those they have been gifted to lead. The people are the heartbeat of the organization and will either make or break its success. With this scenario, we see that the *why* within the organization has not changed, and the expectations for the members within the organization remain the same.

Questions to consider:

- How would it be easier (or harder) to focus on leadership when you don't have to manage shareholders' expectations?

- What are the similarities and differences between leading in industry and leading in the military?

Example 3: A Time *of* Change—Addressing the Unexpected

The SARS CoV-2 or coronavirus, commonly known as "COVID-19", has caused a pandemic affecting millions of people throughout the United States and the world. In response, our country's leadership recommended that the economy shut down and citizens remain at home except for those identified as essential personnel. The aim of this approach, along with social distancing, sought to ensure that medical facilities could accommodate the expected wave of virus patients and allow for a more manageable strategy to defeat it. Times had indeed changed.

Leadership based on margins and numbers appeared to be less relevant as the customer base, and associated processes or procedures, became the focal point. Organizations first had to restore consumer confidence and trust (assuming those existed before) in this new reality before considering margins and profits. Leadership focused on the people was also in question because social-distancing requirements had a direct impact on social gatherings in the workplace and the conventional processes used to run an organization.

Leaders were now forced to focus on their employees' and customers' health and safety for the good of both the organization and the individual. Where so many organizations had come to view employees as commodities or, in harsher terms, those who contributed to the organization's personnel costs, they must now be considered vulnerable human beings. They are the ones who keep the doors open. Without them, leadership is no longer required.

Takeaway: As a noun, "leadership" can be defined as leading a group of people or an organization. Thus, if an organization must close due to the economy or a pandemic, we might suspect that leadership is a moot point. So perhaps leadership is more than just an act of leading? As a verb, "leading" can be defined as influencing people by providing purpose, direction, and motivation. Perhaps it is a calling from within to make things better— to affect change instead of being affected by it? This calling from within becomes the passion driving a leader to be bolder and seek to make a difference. It becomes that *why* they do what they do, which leads them to the crossroads of how to approach this passion for leading with joy. Finding and recognizing joy will have a positive impact on the lives of those whom they serve and who will follow them.

When the unexpected happens, it is not uncommon for human beings at every level to refocus on those things deemed important. It is frequently the scene, after a tornado or hurricane, when someone who has lost nearly everything sifts through the rubble to find meaningful photos and comment that they are thankful to be alive. They reflect on the importance of loved ones and friends. In other words, when we remove all the material and monetary things in our lives, what matters are the relationships that define us.

The COVID-19 pandemic brought to the forefront our need for relationships, social interaction, and a renewed appreciation for our loved ones and friends. The news and social media highlighted pictures of family members visiting loved ones in nursing homes and talking through the windows. We saw many birthday or graduation celebrations with loved one's parading by in their cars, honking to demonstrate their affection and admiration. Human beings need social interaction, friendship, and recognition. Perhaps the silver lining of this terrible pandemic is a newfound realization of our need for interaction with one another. Those who choose to lead must be mindful of their reasons for taking on this role, and the importance of relationships and interactions.

Questions to consider:

- Is leadership an "act," or is it a social inter "act" ion? (Consider different leadership theories: authoritative, transactional, transformational, servant, etc.)

- Is leadership situational or based on consistent principles that can be applied to every situation?

Making the Decision: Acknowledging Your Leadership "*Why*"? and Sticking to It!

There are many reasons why people seek leadership positions. As depicted in the first example, they may do so to assume control and redirect the organization. This move may stem from their own initiative or be at the request of the board of directors or shareholders. The key to understanding this example is the shift in focus for the organization. The *why*, or initial reasons or culture attracting employees and customers, was sacrificed under this redirection. In certain circumstances, regaining control or redirecting may be a requirement for an organization's basic survival. Still, this example suggests that, when an organization no longer resonates with its purpose, the organization suffers.

The second example depicted a changing of the guard resulting from a leader's past performance and the benefits of their career advancement. What stands out here is the consistent focus on the organization from both leaders: the old and the new. Leaders are—first and foremost—there for the betterment of the organization and its members as opposed to themselves or the shareholders. The organization's purpose must continue to be strengthened and the incoming leader is hired to build on the predecessor's success. This changing of the guard is an opportunity for reflection on the impact leadership has had on the organization and the opportunity to build on those shared reflections.

The third example suggests how an event, or a time *of* change, can be the catalyst for a switch in leadership. The COVID-19 pandemic dramatically changed circumstances for nearly every human being on the globe. From businesses being temporarily shut down to those reorganizing to accommodate social distancing, leaders at every level were faced with addressing these unforeseen situations. Leadership required a focus on employees as much as on the bottom line, with the federal government incentivizing organizations that retained their employees to keep the economy afloat.

This funding support required a renewed focus on employees as essential to both the organization and the economy. Thus, the government induced a new *why* for every organization that took advantage of the stimulus— now the jobs that supported an organization became just as important as the organization's services. Perhaps this strikes a critical point for every leader or would-be leader to consider. Without people to lead, leadership is not required.

Leaders must know their reasons for leading and they must be accountable for those reasons. Followers do not always get to choose their leaders, but leaders do decide to lead. It has been said that our reputation is how others view us and our character is who we really are. Without knowing *why* you lead and who you are as a leader, the chances are who you really are and who people think you are will not be the same.

Takeaway: Understanding why we choose to lead and knowing who we really are become catalysts for deriving joy from our work. Research suggests that recognizing our role, talents, and contributions can stimulate joy in the workplace.[5] If you don't know why you are in the position you are in and who you are, regarding your strengths and weaknesses, it is doubtful you will experience joy in your position.

---

5 Moldoveanu, M., & Narayandas, D. (2019). The future of leadership development. Harvard Business Review, 97(2), 40–48.

At this point, you are probably thinking—leadership is a dynamic process requiring attention to both employees and the bottom line—and you would be correct. The critical point of this discussion is the revelation of *why* you lead. To adequately address both employees and the bottom line requires a leader who knows who they are and why they are there.

When leaders know why they lead, and they are transparent within the organization as to who they are, the difference between reputation and character is minimized. Additionally, the stress to maintain one's reputation is reduced and finding joy in leadership has the opportunity to surface. Regardless of the reason for change, understanding who we are and why we seek leadership positions are fundamental when dealing with the inherent challenges and dangers, both foreseen and unforeseen, that will confront us as leaders, as we shall discuss more in Part II.

Questions to consider:

- Why do you, or would you, choose a leadership position?

- Why is it essential for you to know the reason for choosing the position?

- How does understanding your reason for choosing a leadership position make it easier to deal with the challenges that you will confront as a leader?

Part I Recap:
Why People Seek Leadership Positions;
Making the Decision

- There are many different reasons why people seek leadership positions.

- Knowing and conveying those reasons is important to both the leader and the people in the organization.

- Change within the organization is a constant that must always be considered when approaching the leadership challenge. Thus, the consistency of knowing why we lead can provide stability during these times of change.

- Leaders must decide where to focus their attention: employee development and growth or business bottom line. Their reason for leading must coincide with this choice.

Part II:

The Inherent Challenges and Dangers that Lie Ahead

From those early days of being selected as captain to choose the dodgeball team, it became clear there was (and always will be) inherent friction in being a leader. Perhaps this is because leaders must choose, communicate with, and organize a group of human beings toward a common goal or vision. The only difference between the dodgeball captain and an organization's CEO is that the choices, communications, and expectations within the group become more complex—or do they? Perhaps what changes over time is our approach to leadership. Our youth's innocence is often replaced with the perceived *correctness* of our views as reflected in our choices, communications, and expectations. We quickly forget the purity of candor displayed in youth.

I remember being in the tiny airport terminal in Tyler, Texas, and walking past two young boys playing in the gate area waiting to fly with their parents. As I passed them, the younger brother looked at his older brother and said out loud, "that man has a big nose!" I couldn't help but smile, and I looked at him and said, "Yes, I do, thank you for noticing!" Ah yes, the purity of youth! Young children's innocence is to be cherished because they speak frankly without any filters or malicious intent. Being politically correct is just the opposite and it is not genetic—it's a learned behavior.

Unfortunately, in today's politically correct world, choices, communications, and expectations often become convoluted and confused. Matter-of-factly speaking is often avoided for fear of being accused of saying the wrong thing. Leaders quickly learn that everything they say and do can be subject to immediate scrutiny in today's social media-focused world. This makes dealing with the *inherent challenges* of transparent communications, relational expectations, personal and professional growth, and ownership much more difficult to navigate.

Consequently, a leader will instead choose the path of least resistance, adopting a directive or autocratic approach while avoiding complex challenges, but this only serves to create more problems over time. The approach involves a shift from leading a group of people or an organization to managing behaviors to ensure the bottom line or, more likely, the leader's survival. This shift ignores the *selfless*, human nature requirements of the employee-focused organization and resorts to a *selfish* self-centered approach. The result is a culture filled with the *inherent dangers* of power, prestige, and position. I refer to these as "dangers" because they can completely undermine the altruistic progress that authentic leadership can make.

Second only to knowing ourselves and why we choose to lead, understanding the inherent challenges and dangers most leaders face is essential to making the journey pleasurable. Ironically, none of them are entirely new to leadership, its theories, or processes. What *is* a *new* leadership consideration, though, is to understand them in the context of finding joy in leadership, as opposed to merely surviving the experience.

Challenges

Transparent Communications

Communications within an organization are complex and often involve more than just two parties—the sender and the receiver. Those at the top must assume that all their communications will be shared throughout the organization. Also, they must never discount the water fountain discussions and the impact that behind-the-scenes conversations can have on the organization, as the following story shows:

David was a top performer in the organization. He was mainly hired for his extensive network of relationships within the information technology services community. But he interviewed extremely well and hit the ground running, establishing several potential clients within the first few months of joining the company. Everyone seemed thrilled to have David on the team, but things started to change after about six months.

Mary entered the CEO's office and asked if he had a moment to talk. The CEO believed in an open-door policy and welcomed the opportunity to listen to concerns. Mary suggested that there was some friction building among the team members and David. David would do the rounds through the small business offices, sowing discontent by having closed-door conversations complaining about other team members, the management, and the leadership.

According to Mary, David displayed a can-do team attitude when in his supervisor's presence but a completely different one when among his teammates. Mary felt this two-sided approach had an impact on morale, because several of his co-workers had discussed the matter with her and encouraged her to raise it with the CEO. The CEO thanked Mary for her honesty and said he would speak to David.

This story raises some interesting yet typical communication challenges. The CEO follows an open-door policy, encouraging honesty and transparency within the organization, and yet that same honesty and transparency are not replicated throughout. Mary was not afraid to share her concerns with the CEO, but she could not have a similar awkward conversation directly with David, her peer. This example shows how employees will often tolerate a situation they may disagree with just to avoid conflict. Rather than confronting it, they "escalate it" to the next level.

Avoiding conflict and difficult conversations erodes accountability within an organization. When this is absent between members of the organization, it becomes difficult to establish trust. Without trust, open communication is difficult at best. The case is clear: Mary did not trust David because his behavior was inconsistent. Instead of risking an awkward conversation with him, she passed the problem on to the CEO.

Takeaway: Leadership communication challenges within an organization exist at every level. It's simply not enough for the leader to articulate the *why* of the organization. This is an inherent leadership challenge because the consistency of the *why* must be continuously communicated and modeled by all members of the organization. Leaders must mentor those they lead to face and candidly address concerns with their peers and supervisors alike. Therefore, transparent communication is an ever-present challenge requiring consistent daily attention and encouragement. Without it, leaders are likely to inherit issues that could—and should—have been resolved at a lower level, effectively replacing any joy or personal achievement with strife.

The CEO walked down the hall and knocked on David's door, asking if he had a moment to talk. He started by sharing how pleased he was to have brought him into the team, and at how David had expanded the client and opportunity base in a short six months. When he had hired David, the CEO had shared the vision and the *why* behind the company's existence. He had stressed to David the importance of a team effort so that—if we took care of others in the team and were accountable to each other—the rest would take care of itself. He reiterated these same points to David a little more directly this time to ensure that he got the message and he then asked for feedback on how things were going.

From that first selection in dodgeball through every personnel selection a leader makes, dealing with human beings and their feelings is omni-present. It is frequently stated that leaders and supervisors spend 90% of their time on 10% of their employees. This statement has been used so often that it has become a foregone conclusion.

The downside of this foregone conclusion is a leader is accepting that 90% of the organization will be ignored at the expense of the high-maintenance 10%. A better way to look at it is how can we better communicate with the 10% to get them back on board and so enhance the 90% already there? In most cases, every person is hired in the expectation that they will improve the team, and every person accepts the position in the expectation that the job will provide for their work-related needs. Thus, leaders must continuously assess the byproduct of their communications—both sides' perceived expectations.

Typically, communication at the time of hire was meant to be clear enough to create appropriate and complementary expectations for both employer and employee. And, ideally, further open and consistent communication within the organization should clarify and reinforce those expectations. Yet another inherent leadership challenge is to ensure that the leader's expectations are clear to the follower and the follower's expectations clear to the leader. This mutual understanding engenders accountability and trust.

Questions to consider:

- When an employee, like David, is engaging in potentially damaging behind-the-scenes discussions, where have communications broken down (with colleagues like Mary, the CEO, policies and procedures, etc.)?

- If you had been in the CEO's position, would you have handled the situation differently? If so, how?

Relational Expectations

David thanked the CEO for coming by, appreciated the feedback, and said how nice it was to be a part of the team. He mentioned that several of the leads he had brought to the organization appeared to be positive, and that a few of them were already discussing partnerships for future opportunities. He suggested that he had been working with his teammates to get their buy-in for these potential partnerships and was excited about the possibilities.

The CEO asked David if he had perceived any dissension or "pushback" that might impede these potential partnerships and opportunities. David replied that he was still adjusting to some of the policies and procedures within the organization but did not anticipate anything impeding his progress toward securing this new business. The CEO thanked David for his time and said he looked forward to hearing more. But the real question in the CEO's mind was whether his expectations were fully accepted and understood by David.

Another inherent challenge for leaders and—quite frankly organizations—is understanding relational expectations from both sides. It appears clear that Mary's expectations are different from David's, and that the CEO's expectations for those within the organization are not as straightforward and transparent as he may have thought. The reality is that articulating and refining expectations are part of a continuous cycle of communicating and assessing. Sharing the overall vision—the *why* behind the company—is not limited to the hiring process: full (and sustained) understanding needs a continuing conversation adapted to each employee and their personal responsibility for addressing daily challenges and potential conflicts.

In most cases, conflict centers around the tension between the shift from selfishness to selflessness. As mentioned earlier, David's appointment was influenced by his extensive network of relationships within the IT services community. From the organization's perspective, David would be a "good fit" to grow its business (a selfish desire). David, on the other hand, accepted this new opportunity confident that he would bring value to the organization while also being appropriately compensated and promoted within the firm (a selfish desire).

Obviously, there were some selfless motives in both cases: the organization giving David a job and David helping the organization grow. The primary point is that without a clear mutual understanding of relational expectations, within both conflict and harmony, it is difficult to develop the trust and accountability within the organization to ensure the transformation from selfish to selfless attitude and behavior. In the aviation community, this transformation is facilitated through briefings and debriefings to address expectations and ensure that all participants are in agreement, as illustrated in the following story.

Whether flying a single-seat fighter aircraft in formation with three other planes or flying a large commercial aircraft with a crew of seven, understanding relational expectations can be a life or death issue. We need only reflect on the flight deemed the "miracle on the Hudson" on January 15, 2009. On this day, an Airbus 320 under the command of Captain Chesley Burnett Sullenberger III safely landed in the Hudson River minutes after hitting a flock of geese shortly after take-off from New York's La Guardia airport. There was no time to establish or debate expectations: takeoff to touchdown in the Hudson was under five minutes.

Before loading passengers in a commercial aircraft, the captain briefs the entire crew on the weather, aircraft status, routing, and any unique issues that need to be discussed. There are standard operating procedures for each crew position, and any expected deviations to those standard procedures are addressed. Finally, the captain asks each crew member if there are any questions or points for clarification before completing the briefing. When the briefing is finished, expectations are clear, and the entire crew is in agreement, just as they were on January 15, 2009. When Captain Sullenberger called to the flight attendants and told them they were making an emergency landing in the Hudson, there was no discussion and everyone did their job as expected.

Takeaway: Ensuring that an entire organization is "on the same page" requires repeated engagement and two-way conversations to maintain clear understanding and trust on both sides. Communication must be frequent enough to address changes from the previous talk and any unique circumstances for the update. What makes relational expectations an inherent leadership challenge is the continuous effort to manage expectations on both sides in order to affect the transition from selfish to selfless. Without a universal shift, the leadership will need to focus on individuals—the outliers—rather than on the team. Finding joy in leadership is directly related to the success of this shift, and occurs when there is a consistent agreement regarding purpose and goals.

When purpose and goals are clearly defined, they can become metrics upon which we can measure performance. With clear and open reminders of the organization's purpose, and a full understanding of how relational expectations fit within that purpose, we can assess performance from both a personal and professional perspective. Thus, a third challenge leaders must face to find joy in leadership is ensuring personal and professional growth through performance.

Questions to consider:

- How does the two-way feedback in communication fit into the relational expectations process?

- Why is it essential for leaders to understand their employee's expectations?

Personal and Professional Growth

Leaders must take the time to understand the personal and professional goals of those who report directly to them in order to assess their unique skill sets and ambitions. When followers feel they can contribute and make an impact, they enjoy a sense of engagement and appreciation, as shown in the following story.

Mark knocked on his supervisor's door and asked if she had a moment? She said, of course, and invited him to close the door and sit down. He had only just joined the organization—nine months ago, right out of college, where he had graduated with honors. He was an enthusiastic employee with a lot of energy, ideas, and passion.

His supervisor (Sally) started the conversation off, asking Mark how things were going and what was on his mind. Mark said he was doing fine but was curious about what had happened to some of the suggestions he had offered during their initial feedback session. At that time, Mark had brought up the possibility of moving to a four-day workweek to achieve a better work–life balance. Also, Mark told her that he was keen to fill the open manager's position that had just opened up two weeks ago. The previous manager in this position had been with the company for 20 years.

The highlight of this story is that dealing with personal and professional growth as a leader involves an understanding of the different generations within the workplace. The current workforce consists of Baby Boomers, Generation X, and Millennials, with Generation Z just beginning to enter the workforce. It is predicted that, by 2025, 75% of the global workforce will be Millennials,[6] and, clearly, the personal and professional growth expectations for Baby Boomers and Generation X are very different from those for Millennials.

Millennials are often negatively characterized as narcissistic, privileged, and lacking in work ethic.

6 Phillips, R. (2020). *The Perception of Mutual Accountability within the LMX: Its Influence on the Supervisor and Employee Relationship*. A dissertation presented in partial fulfillment of the requirements for the degree Doctorate of Philosophy, Grand Canyon University, Phoenix, Arizona.

However, on the positive side, they are creative, technically savvy, frugal, socially aware, and very accepting.[7] We need only spend time with World War II generation members to hear similar negative adjectives to describe Baby Boomers. The point is that every generation that follows the previous one will often be described in terms less flattering than those they would express themselves, and vice versa. Nonetheless, progress and excellence continue to surface.

Mark represented the Millennial stereotype well, reflecting his attitude, expectations, and preferences to his supervisor. Predictably, Millennials wish to participate in decisions on general aspects of their organization. In other words, they want to feel as though they are making a difference, given the time they spend at work. Similarly, this generation is incredibly environmentally conscious. Whether we believe in climate change or not, Millennials tend to be passionate about taking care of their environment—indeed a noble cause. The consistency with which they attend to the areas they believe in is undoubtedly energy to be harnessed and grown.

Sally replied that she had been thinking about Mark's suggestions and was looking forward to discussing them with him. Regarding the first proposal of changing to a four-day workweek, she asked Mark if he had discussed the idea

7 Andersen, O. J., & Torsteinsen, H. (2017). "The Master of the House"—Agencies in municipal service provision: Balancing autonomy and accountability. *Administration & Society*, 49(5), 730–752. doi:10.1177/0095399714555749

with his colleagues and considered any potential impact on their customer base. She said that, while this appeared to be a potential work–life balance solution on the surface, such a move had to consider all effects both inside and outside the organization.

Takeaway: Understanding personal and professional growth from a generational perspective is an inherent challenge for leaders across all staff in the workplace. Without taking a generational view into account, leaders may assume that they know their employees' personal and professional growth needs but instead miss the mark, creating problems for both themselves and others in the organization. Understanding generational behavior and motivations is essential when considering and discussing personal and professional growth opportunities.

As a result of Sally's interaction, Mark recognized that a few other considerations needed to be addressed before a decision could be made on the four-day workweek issue. Sally went on to the next question—the management position. She pointed out that the right person for the position would need to be someone who demonstrated the ability to understand and address different personnel issues within the manager's sphere of influence.

Mark quickly recognized that there was much more to both these issues than he had previously realized. He told Sally that he would discuss the idea of a four-day workweek with his colleagues, taking into account potential impacts on their customers. He was excited to have the chance to contribute to this potential work–life balance solution and hoped the opportunity might help to prepare him for a management position in the future.

This situation gave Sally the chance to offer Mark a personal and professional growth experience that she could measure and assess. During their short discussion, Mark's communication skills, relational expectations, growth potential, and now ownership were evident, as demonstrated by his willingness to vet the four-day workweek idea. Encouraging employee ownership is the fourth inherent challenge of leadership and vital to the experience of joy in the process.

Questions to consider:

- Why is it such a challenge for leaders to understand personal and professional goals for their employees?

- What are the advantages to the organization when they do?

Ownership

In the aviation world, an aspiring pilot's first solo flight is a significant event. From the beginning to the end of the flight, the pilot owns every decision and its consequences. They have a network of support around them to help in the decision-making process but, ultimately, they own the execution. The entire learning process up to this point prepares them for this event.

When fledgling aviators enter the "Learn to Fly Here" doors, transparent communications are offered to discuss the process, the requirements, and the costs. Once an instructor is assigned, relational expectations are articulated and will continue to be refined throughout the learning experience. Each lesson has professional growth expectations, and truly gifted instructors will ensure that these expectations align with personal growth. The entire process feeds the ownership and trust that both parties expect to be present before the first solo flight.

Takeaway: The inherent challenge of ownership revolves around the leader's role of mentoring through communication, expectation, and the move toward empowerment. Without these three precursors, ownership and empowerment are routinely absent. As in the aviation example, ownership typically culminates when the leader has provided the appropriate instruction, guidance, and expectations while at the same time ensuring the required growth and performance to enable empowerment and ownership.

In Mark's case, his supervisor recognized that he needed more growth and experience before he would be ready to assume and take ownership of a management role. What makes this an inherent leadership challenge is the deliberate investment of time a leader must take to develop their followers like Mark. Ownership, like empowerment, is not a single act by the leader. It is the process of promoting a mind shift in the follower whereby they no longer need to be told or prompted to act. The follower develops an attitude of ownership and accountability, reflecting the change in mind shift and giving the leader confidence to know that the follower now owns it.

While the instructor may be confident that the new pilot is ready to take ownership, when they send the student out for their initial solo, they always feel some natural anxiety. This is an important point because this entire process revolves around trust. A leader must trust that they have appropriately mentored and instructed their student and be confident that the student has absorbed their mentoring and guidance. When a follower knows that a leader has placed a special trust in them, they typically strive to ensure that the leader is not disappointed.

The inherent challenges of transparent communications, relational expectations, personal and professional growth, and ownership are critical to developing the trust essential to finding joy in leadership. However, juxtaposed with these inherent challenges are three dangers inhibiting one's recognition and acknowledgement of the joy of leadership. These dangers are power, prestige, and position.

Questions to consider:

- Why is it essential for leaders to develop ownership in their followers?

- How would you, as a leader, develop and maintain ownership in your followers?

Dangers

Addressing the inherent challenges of leadership just discussed requires a selfless approach to leadership that focuses on the follower and their development toward further ownership in the organization. This approach develops trust within the relationship, and serves to enhance transparency, expectation, growth, and ownership. Frequently, this selfless approach generates success, and with success comes prestige, along with a reputation for results, both within and outside the organization.

Developing a reputation for positive influence based on past successes feels good and reinforces leaders' belief in themselves. Most leaders set out with the vision of making a positive difference within their community and their organization by the services and jobs they offer. With success comes recognition and with recognition comes newfound respect. But, before long, the vision can expand dangerously to preserve the leader's perceived reputation as they come to believe that there is no limit to the influence and impact they can have.

Takeaway: If this success and growing recognition continue for an extended period, they can give the impression that the organization only succeeds because of its leader. The phrase "success breeds success" can then begin to go to the leader's head. The fundamentals that brought success in the first place can be replaced with feelings associated with all the three leadership dangers: power, prestige, and position. I call these "dangers" because they tend to create division and shift the *selfless* focus on the organization and its followers to the *selfish* pursuits of the leader. Sadly, this insidious process often robs the leader of finding joy in leadership.

Questions to consider:

- Within the context of transitioning from selfish to selfless, why does the phrase "success breeds success" invite the dangers of power, prestige, and position?

- Why are power, prestige, and position considered dangers and not challenges?

Power

With over two decades as either President or Prime Minister, it would be fair to say that Vladimir Putin has a powerful influence on Russia's people. Forbes highlighted that Putin was "voted the world's most powerful person four times between 2013 and 2016"[8]. This reputation for power influences not only the psyche of the leader but their followers as well.

As the perception of power grows, so does the need to maintain the perception. Research suggests that leaders with power motives tend to foster relationships with those who promote their power interests.[9] The selfless focus on those being led is replaced with a selfish focus on those relationships that maintain or enhance their power. Leadership is no longer focused on the leader's impact on the follower but instead on their perceived power.[10]

When this happens, the relationship's influence shifts to the follower who is striving to gain favor and acceptance from the leader. Their focus shifts from their own development to providing support and allegiance to the leader. Their vision changes from one focused on the organization to one focused on sustaining or enhancing the leader's power. Organizational visions are subtly redesigned to support the reign of the leader.

Takeaway: The danger here is that the focus remains on the leader—ensuring or enhancing their power. It deflects from the organization's original vision, which was to develop future leaders. If success breeds success, perhaps the same can be true of power: power breeds more power to quench an unquenchable thirst.

---

8 Rogers, J. (2020, June 13). As Russia launches new nuclear submarine, Putin makes case for staying in power. *Forbes.* https://www.forbes.com/profile/vladimir-putin/#2a561ad66fc5

9 Lee, K., Chae, Y., & Shin, I. (2016). Motivational antecedents of leader-member exchange differentiation: Evidence from South Korea. *Asia Pacific Journal of Management*, 33(1), 87–112. doi:10.1007/s10490-015-9454-8

10 Krause, D. (2015). Four types of leadership and orchestra quality. *Nonprofit Management & Leadership*, 25(4), 431–447. doi:10.1002/nml.21132

Eventually, the needs of the individual follower are suppressed, and leadership becomes autocratic rule.

When leadership shifts from guiding to controlling, the foundation and vision of the organization are compromised. As we observed in the first example in Part I, "A Time *to* Change," the successful small business owner reorganized the company to focus on revenue instead of the original integrity-focused vision. This power move eventually cost the organization its reputation and customer base—ironically, defeating the revenue-generating purpose for the change in the first place.

Questions to consider:

- What are some of the early clues that power is encroaching on leadership?

- When may power be beneficial to the leadership role?

Prestige

Watching a reporter interview a star athlete or Hollywood movie star about current political issues, we realize that those esteemed for their past achievements are assumed to have some expertise in the area they are discussing. Often their opinions carry weight but are baseless because they have no expertise on the subject, only an *esteemed opinion.*

In October 2019, Lebron James was asked about the Houston Rockets General Manager Daryl Morey's

Twitter post supporting Hong Kong's quest for human rights. He stated that Morey was "misinformed or not really educated"[11]. James's response sparked outrage in Hong Kong and highlighted how commenting on issues beyond one's expertise can have an impact on one's reputation and wider realm of influence.

Practically speaking, we would suspect that Lebron James had no desire to spark outrage in Hong Kong. In fact, he probably never intended to come across as insulting to the Rockets General Manager. He and his teammates had recently returned from playing two exhibition games in China and it would seem that this experience had influenced his perspective. My intent here is not to judge James's comments but to highlight the dangers of prestige.

Takeaway: With success comes notoriety, and with notoriety comes the perception of expertise among those deemed leaders within their industries. The attention this brings can become addictive and, as with any addiction, it can become harmful to our leadership and those we influence. Today's extensive social media environment makes navigating the dangers of prestige and notoriety even more challenging.

Leaders with large followings often feel compelled to address the concerns of their followers. If a leader loses sight of their vision and area of expertise,

---

11 Golliver, B. (2019, October 15). Lebron James draws scrutiny for comments critical of Daryl Morey's Hong Kong tweet. *The Washington Post.* https://www.washingtonpost.com/ sports/2019/10/15/lebron-james-criticizes-daryl-moreys-decision-send-controversial-hong-kong-tweet

they can quickly be drawn into matters contrary to their character and potentially harmful to their reputations. Prestige can be an insidious danger, causing leaders to be sidetracked and robbed of the joy that brought them their success in the first place.

Questions to consider:

- When could it be beneficial for someone to speak outside their realm of influence?

- How do social media platforms promote the opinions of celebrities and industry leaders outside their areas of expertise?

Position

Finally, it is essential to consider the influence a position or title can have on a leader. We see too often that politicians who have served for decades lose sight of their elected responsibilities. Instead of representing their constituents, they often become addicted to their own identity and power. This causes them to shift from representing and caring for those they serve to focusing instead on preserving their own position and status. When most of us have been in a job for a significant amount of time, we start to feel entitled to that position and even future promotions, as illustrated in the following story.

Fran walked humbly into the Chairman of the Board's office and took a seat behind the large oak desk. The Chairman had good news for

Fran: she would be the company's new CEO. He complimented her on 15 years of unfailing dedication, professionalism, and loyalty to everyone she had worked for and with. She was clearly deserving of this leadership opportunity.

Fran was selected from among her peers, competing with Jon and Carolyn. Jon had been with the company for 20 years and believed he would be the heir apparent to the position. His record was nearly flawless, yet several coworkers in the company voiced concerns about him being in charge. Carolyn also interviewed for the job and, having been with the company for 15 years, she too was a strong candidate. Fran was chosen because she possessed the right balance of expertise (via previous ownership and growth) and relational skills (via communication and relational expectations).

Takeaway: Selection for a leadership position must be executed carefully, considering each candidate's personality and motives. Positions of authority can, and sadly are, periodically abused. Those who look perfect on paper may not be as perfect as they look. For leaders to be effective, they must positively affect the lives of those they lead. When a potential leader is more interested in the position's rank and title outside their office than creating a culture for their employees' success, the promotion can be a catalyst for poor leadership.

Leadership is a privilege, not an entitlement. We can strive to be considered for a leadership position, but time in grade doesn't entitle us to lead a group or an organization. Leadership is not—and can never be—a one-way interaction. The nature of dealing with other human beings makes leadership relational, and effective leadership requires gauging both sides of the relationship in an ongoing process of trust and influence.[12]

This two-way interaction is wrought with the inherent challenges and dangers previously discussed, so it must be approached deliberately and purposefully with a full understanding of *who* we are and *why* we lead. Not everyone is wired or equipped to lead effectively. Yet, sadly, among those who are, many still fail to find joy in their leadership. By understanding the basics of human behavior and interaction, it becomes clear that joy must be pursued and we will examine this at greater depth in Part III.

Questions to consider:

- How will knowing these challenges and dangers have an impact on your approach to leadership?

- How have these challenges and dangers had an impact on you as a leader or follower in the past?

---

12 Crawford, J. A., & Kelder, J. A. (2018). Do we measure leadership effectively? Articulating and evaluating scale development psychometrics for best practice. *Leadership Quarterly*, 30, 133–144. doi:10.1016/j.leaqua.2018.07.001

Part II Recap:
The Inherent Challenges and Dangers that Lie Ahead

- In today's politically correct world, leadership choices, communications, and expectations may often become convoluted and confused.
- *Communication* is an ever-present challenge requiring consistent daily attention and encouragement.
- Ensuring that the entire organization is "on the same page" requires repeated *relational engagement* and two-way conversations to maintain clear understanding and trust on both sides.
- Understanding *personal and professional growth* from a generational perspective is an inherent challenge for leaders that touches on all generations in the workplace.
- The inherent challenge of *ownership* revolves around the leader's role of mentoring through communications expectation, and growth toward empowerment.
- Successfully navigating the challenges associated with leadership doesn't protect us from the leadership dangers of *power, prestige, and position.*
- Maintaining an awareness of these dangers and their impact on the joy in leadership is our key to avoiding them.

Part III:

Why Isn't Leadership
More Enjoyable?

Dealing with the inherent challenges and dangers of a leadership position is often stressful for even the most seasoned professionals. Think about the many pictures you have seen of United States presidents' faces comparing them at the beginning and end of their term. You can see clearly how much a president ages during their time in office. Each one faces immense challenges, endless work hours, competing interests, and the responsibility for the good of the country at an intense level every day. In a less concentrated manner, business leaders deal with the competing interests of taking care of their employees and satisfying their bosses' expectations. Their daily stress level inevitably takes its toll and often robs them of the joy in the experience of leadership, as illustrated below.

Mike, the company's CEO, returned to the office after meeting with the President to go over the last quarter's figures. Despite increasing sales by 10% and growing the client base by successfully winning two new contracts, Mike had not met the quarterly goals he had set three months before. During this period, his human resources and domestic sales directors had left to pursue new opportunities. This had significantly increased the demands on Mike, causing him to feel overwhelmed, and he began to question whether this leadership opportunity was worth the stress and anxiety.

Takeaway: Leadership is not for everyone. In Part I, we discussed a few reasons why people accept leadership positions and highlighted the importance of understanding these reasons. In Part II, we discussed the inherent challenges and dangers associated with being a leader. Knowing why you accepted the leadership position, and the challenges and dangers that lie ahead, is no recipe for success—nor, indeed, any guarantee of enjoying the experience along the way.

To achieve excellence in any endeavor, we must pursue aspirations similar to those of top-level athletes. We need only consider those labeled "The Greatest of All Time" within their respective sports to realize that they had mastered the fundamentals of their game.

When Michael Jordan was labeled one of the greatest offensive players of all time, he shifted gears to achieve the same as a defensive player. When Tiger Woods decided to take his game to the next level, he worked on the fundamentals of his already near-perfect swing to make it better. Achieving the level of *greatest* in perfection is a quest few genuinely strive for, but those who never give up in its pursuit do achieve that accolade in their profession.

Author Jeff Olson summed it up well: "Successful people do what unsuccessful people are not willing to do."[13] To be a successful leader requires perseverance to master the most important fundamentals of human behavior and interaction:

- understanding the problems people face;
- adopting a positive attitude toward problem-solving;
- maintaining a far-sighted perspective;
- addressing conflicting demands from both sides; and
- not losing sight of *why* one leads.

Each of these fundamentals must be mastered if a leader wishes to find joy in leadership. To neglect any one of them is to settle for something less for both leaders and their followers.

Questions to consider:

- What is the impact on the organization of a leader who is always stressed out?

---

13 Olson, J. (2013). *The slight edge*. Greenleaf Book Group.

- What are the benefits to the organization and the leader when joy is evident?

Dealing with the Problems People Face

People are complex creatures influenced by their upbringing and experiences. When they enter the workplace, they must engage with others in very different circumstances and situations, each with their own fears and trepidations rooted in their need for affirmation and security. Sigmund Freud described this need as "transference," whereby we seek to repeat in our adult relationships what we *either received or were denied* during our childhood.[14]

Combine the need for affirmation and security with our inherent selfish nature and it is no surprise that, when two or more people are involved in a task, there is a high probability of conflict. Leaders cannot avoid dealing with such problems. But, when they realize that the nature of human interaction revolves around fundamental human needs, the task becomes manageable.

Remember the conflict between Mary and David described in Part II? David made the rounds through the small business offices, sowing discontent by having closed-door conversations with his coworkers complaining about other team members, the management, and the leadership. Ironically, if we had interviewed coworkers from David's previous jobs, we would have found almost identical behavior.

14 Raelin, J. A. (2016). It's not about the leaders: It's about the practice of leadership. *Organizational Dynamics*, 45(2), 124–131. doi:10.1016/j.orgdyn.2016.02.006

66

What makes David's case even more interesting is that he is gifted and thriving as a business developer. He is exceptionally cordial with clients, creates strong rapport among teammates, and shows meticulous attention to detail. So what is driving him to sow such discontent in the workplace? Short of using Freud's psychoanalytic approach to determining unconscious thoughts and motivations, it can be assumed David has some difficulties with affirmation and security.

For example, trust is a factor in David's relationship with his coworkers. Because he doesn't trust them, he isn't sure that they accept him in his new position and he fears that they may undermine his efforts. He spends time figuring out whether his coworkers accept him by trying to identify those who may be a threat to him within the organization. This search for affirmation and security is not only counterproductive to generating synergy in the organization: it also takes up time that could be used to grow the team and business.

Developing trust within an organization, in order to counteract the inevitability of interpersonal conflict, is directly related to the inherent leadership challenges discussed in Part II. Research suggests that interpersonal trust is an expectation or belief that future actions will be helpful or favorable to one's interests.[15] We all want something out of a relationship and we are hopeful that we will be better off for it—a prospect that reflects our inherent selfish desires.

---

15 Ullah, S., Hasnain, S. A., Khalid, A., Aslam, A., & Zealand, N. (2019). Effects of perception of organizational politics on employees' well-being: The mediating role of trust and interpersonal conflicts. *European Online Journal of Natural and Social Sciences*, 8(1), 1–14.

To minimize these selfish desires, leaders need to address all the four challenges described in Part II: transparent communications, relational expectations, personal and professional growth, and ownership. Fortunately, as we shall see in some detail in Parts V and VI, doing so has a positive impact on interpersonal trust and also enhances accountability throughout an organization.

Takeaway: The inherently complex nature of human beings requires a basic understanding of the need for affirmation and security while also acknowledging our innate selfish desires to control our domains. Leaders must understand and accept this fundamental concept, and be willing to navigate the inherent challenges associated with the problems people face in order to develop the interpersonal trust needed to mitigate them. By putting effort into this, leaders will find joy in a more harmonious and efficient workplace—as will the employees!

What we seek, we typically find. If we are looking for problems, we will never be disappointed. If we are looking for solutions, even though it may take time to find them, they are out there as well. If we seek to find joy in leading others—accepting the fact that we will need to navigate conflict—a positive approach toward problem-solving is critical.

Questions to consider:

- If people are indeed an organization's greatest asset, why do leaders often avoid trying to understand them better?

- Given the cost of employee turnover, how much time (and effort) should a leader invest in addressing this?

A Positive Attitude Toward Problem-solving: Problems or Opportunities?

Let's face it: if employees within organizations could motivate themselves and solve their problems, leaders would not be needed. A leader's primary role is to navigate through difficulties and obstacles, providing the direction toward solutions in order to build a synergistic team. How they view a problem has a direct impact on their effectiveness in identifying potential solutions.

Unfortunately, not all leaders—or people generally—view problems the same way. Some leaders believe in the theory of exposure. This suggests that the more exposure you have to those under your command, the more likely you are to see their points of view and understand their concerns. In other words, if you cannot relate to your followers, you may not perceive a problem as a problem, and even (unintentionally) distance yourself from it and ignore it. The danger here, clearly, is your failure to acknowledge and address it.

Ironically for many, having to deal with problems is a problem in and of itself! Perhaps it is because they perceive problems as unwelcome additions to their workload, or maybe that dealing with problems involves risk that is then associated with a fear of failure. Fear of failure can paralyze ingenuity and innovation, leading to stagnation and an avoidance of problems.[16] When leaders avoid or deny problems, they also miss out on discovering new solutions for the future.

Fortunately for all of us, Thomas Edison was neither problem-nor failure-averse. He embraced problems and some even suggest that he sought them out. With 1,093 US patents and 2,332 patents worldwide for every item that used electricity, it is fair to say that he not only sought out problems but also developed a myriad of solutions: the light bulb, motion-picture machines, music-recording equipment, the X-ray machine, and even the tattoo pen.[17] He believed that failure was a great teacher and that we should never stop learning. In fact, one of his most inspirational quotes is "Our greatest weakness lies in giving up. The most certain way to succeed is always to try just one more time."[18]

Some leaders' inability to try just one more time may be rooted in ego or pride, preventing them from exploring new ideas to address a problem. Dealing with change requires leadership and a willingness to embrace a changing, dynamic environment within which to find new solutions to new problems by breaking away from the past.[19]

16 Friedman, S. (2008). Be a better leader, have a richer life. *Harvard Business Review*, 86(4), 46–48.
17 Daum, K. (2016, February 11). 37 quotes from Thomas Edison that will inspire success. Hardly an hour goes by that you don't use something Thomas Edison invented. On his birthday, you can appreciate not only his products but his inspiration. *INC*. https://www.inc.com/kevin-daum/37-quotes-from-thomas-edison-that-will-bring-out-your-best.html
18 Daum, '37 quotes'.
19 Stehlik, D. (2014). Failure: The impartial executioner of leaders, followers, and their organizations. *Journal of Practical Consulting*, 5(1), 41–52.

Another "Greatest of All Time" athlete is the incredible hockey player Wayne Gretzky. Wayne described the difference between good and great this way, "A good hockey player plays where the puck is. A great hockey player plays where the puck is going to be."[20] He pointed out how greatness requires the dynamics of change whereby you live in the present while anticipating the future and dealing appropriately with your current circumstances.

Takeaway: Opportunity presents itself when circumstances dictate change. Clearly, without problems to solve, there is no need for solutions. Leaders must embrace problems positively so that they encourage ingenuity and innovation—finding reasons why something does not work leads to figuring out how it *will* work. Just like Thomas Edison's approach, leaders must embrace failure as the way to a solution—and appreciate the success this brings.

A tremendous athlete does not earn the moniker "Greatest of All Time" if they are not willing to step into an arena, make mistakes, learn from them, and continue developing through the entire experience. Wayne Gretzky *knew* where the puck was going to be, not because he was psychic but because his intuition based on experience told him so. He played hockey for many years, on thousands of occasions, gradually learning the game's nuances until he was playing with the boldness and savvy that few others have ever since matched.

20 Medruit, F. (2017, December 30). 15 Wayne Gretzky quotes to make you work harder on your goals. https://www.goalcast.com/2017/12/30/wayne-gretzky-quotes

Similarly, the old saying, "There are no old, bold pilots," stands true because old pilots have learned and grown from experiences along the way, and they have developed an intuition to see where an airplane is going before it gets there. Intellectually and physically, they lead their aircraft through the vastness of the skies by completely integrating themselves in their present situation so that they can successfully mitigate or deal with any changes or problems that may arise.

For example, Captain Sullenberger brilliantly exemplifies and demonstrates the power of intuition borne of experience with the "Miracle on the Hudson." What he did was not bold but fully grounded in his past experience and his current intuition, both of which were applied toward a successful outcome in just seconds. Leaders must embrace experiences derived from facing problems head-on with a solution-oriented approach and, in so doing, develop well-founded intuition over time. Thankfully, leaders' responses don't usually need to be accomplished in seconds as in Sully's case. However, leaders do need to be decisive and able to rely confidently on their intuition as problems grow bigger and change becomes more significant.

The COVID-19 pandemic brought about many unforeseen challenges around the world. As each of us stayed at home watching how cities, states, and countries dealt with the matter, it became clear which ones were dealing with the pandemic with a 'here-and-now' focus (where the problem *is*) and which ones were also paying attention to where the pandemic was heading (where the problem *is going to be*). Exceptional leadership and finding joy in leading requires one to welcome problems and see them as opportunities to further develop intuition based on experience. Such intuition, with its focus on the future and in which one can have confidence, helps us to address the third reason why leadership is often less enjoyable than it might be: maintaining a far-sighted perspective.

Questions to consider:

- How do you view problems in the workplace?

- How do you think a leader should encourage their employees to seek out problems and offer innovative solutions?

Maintaining a Far-Sighted Perspective

Whether we see a glass half-empty or half-full may depend on how we start each day. Do you begin your day with inspiration—for example, by reading or meditating on something positive—or by desperation in reacting to the bad news that always seems to headline the newspaper or be the lead story on the morning news? If we are not deliberate and consistent in our daily outlook, it is harder to keep a positive or clear focus. We must address each moment in the context of a consistent long-term vision of seeing our glass half-full.

Tennis is a fascinating sport. What makes it so is the mental toughness (or psyche) of the greatest players. They can be down five games to one in a set yet still maintain their composure and eventually recover to win the match. Creating the winning psyche that this displays involves many factors but begins by focusing on winning the next point despite the game score. This first step toward winning the next point builds to winning the next game, the next set, and eventually the match.

While great leaders cannot aim for success one step at a time, their eyes are always on the far horizon, noting but looking past any obstacles in the here-and-now on their course to future success. President Ronald Reagan had many roles and failures in life before becoming President. He remained fixed on a long-term 'flight plan' and, despite setbacks, he possessed the critical leadership characteristic of keeping one's emotions in check. He often said he would never let things he couldn't do stop him from doing what he could.

Like the great tennis players, President Reagan visualized a future beyond current circumstances, tricky situations, unpopularity and criticism. Instead of succumbing to emotion, he aimed higher for more successes or took shortfalls in his stride with humor. This is the courage of leadership: to take risks, to remain confident in one's intuition, and to remember for oneself the words of the President, "The future does not belong to the light-hearted: it belongs to the brave." The tennis player down by five points can sulk or stand head high—pushing on and suppressing their emotions while foreseeing success.

As human beings, we are all emotional but few of us have mastered the control of our emotions in a regulated way or managed by some other means to offset them. As shown by President Reagan, emotional stability is directly related to the effectiveness of leadership. Research in the past two decades suggests that the emotions leaders display, whether related to their personal traits or the message they are trying to convey, are directly or indirectly linked to their success.[21] Followers look to their leaders for hope and the vision to make hope a reality.

When Captain Tammy Jo Shults' Southwest Boeing 737 had a catastrophic engine failure en route to Dallas, her calm demeanor and strong presence within the cockpit were hailed by the media and commended by the President. When asked how she and her First Officer had been successful in landing the crippled aircraft at Philadelphia International, she attributed it to their training and teamwork. When a leader knows that their actions are always on display and that those within their sphere of influence will respond to those actions, regulating their emotions is essential to meeting the immediate challenge.

As well as managing their emotions, leaders need to take their followers' values and identities into account when they create their visions if they are to communicate these effectively to their followers. A study on cognitive skills and leadership performance found that leaders craft visions to help followers make sense of a situation,

21 Griffith, J., Connelly, S., Thiel, C., & Johnson, G. (2015). How outstanding leaders lead with affect: An examination of charismatic, ideological, and pragmatic leaders. *The Leadership Quarterly*, 26(4), 502–517. doi:10.1016/j.leaqua.2015.03.004

and to avoid any pre-existing obstacles stemming from solutions to problems in the past.[22]

Takeaway: Visualizing success is about recognizing the best in yourself and the best in those you lead, as well as relying on the foundations of your decision-making, training, and experience. Leaders must look beyond the immediate situation to future possibilities, trusting in their people and those processes proven effective in the past. From sports teams, historical battles, or cases of terminal illness, we have all heard stories of those who have succeeded—against all the odds—in achieving the unthinkable.

Maintaining a far-sighted perspective is hard work for a leader. It requires a consistent mindset to look for opportunities among challenges. A quote from the Dalai Lama sums it up nicely:

A positive state of mind is not merely good for you,
It benefits everyone with whom you come in contact,
Literally changing the world.

Visualizing success in the future is a mental outlook that great leaders and athletes develop over time, based on experience and trust in themselves and their team. It requires the mental strength to be fully aware of and accept one's circumstances, knowing that they are part of the solution to a successful outcome. The study on cognitive skills and leadership performance referred

22 Mumford, M., Todd, E., & Higgs, T. (2017). Cognitive skills and leadership performance: The nine critical skills. *The Leadership Quarterly*, 28(1), 24–39. doi:10.1016/j.leaqua.2016.10.012

to earlier described visualizing success as making sense by "framing problem solutions with respect to others and their needs"[23]. Captain Shults clearly understood her situation when the primary engine of her aircraft catastrophically failed en route to Dallas. She was well aware of the expectations of her First Officer as they coordinated efforts to land safely, and she also understood the safety needs of all the passengers on board.

The calm of a leader's demeanor in times of crisis reflects the focus they have on the solution. Thus, finding joy in leadership is directly related to the focus of a leader's perspective. To maintain a far-sighted perspective, the choice is clear: focus on solutions on the horizon to solve problems immediately at hand.

Another obstacle to finding joy is that leaders must satisfy their supervisors while at the same time addressing their followers' needs. As well as understanding their followers' values and identity, leaders must consider the values and identity of those they themselves answer to, as we shall discuss next.

Questions to consider:

- How do you begin each day and where is your focus?

- How can you address the immediate without losing focus on the future?

---

23 Mumford et al., 'Cognitive skills'.

Addressing Demands from Both Sides

The ability to articulate a vision is essential for both employees under a leader's influence and those who supervise and influence the leader. Leaders almost always answer or report to someone. Thus, the challenge is to address all sides of the leadership triangle, as illustrated in the story that follows.

Mike's secretary knocked on the door, came into his office, and informed him that the President had just called and wanted to see Mike in his office right away. Remember Mike from the beginning of this part of the book? He didn't meet his quotas for the past quarter, and he had just lost two critical members of his staff. Being a CEO didn't seem to be all it was cracked up to be, and his leadership challenges were about to become even more stressful.

Mike entered the President's office and sat down in front of his desk. The President greeted him and went directly to the point: the previous quarter's earnings. Indirectly, he let Mike know that he had one more quarter in which to reach or exceed the quarterly goals or there would be leadership changes. The President acknowledged that losing two key staff members was tough and finished the conversation by asking about the hiring status for those positions.

Being in a leadership position is effectively a balancing act between those you answer to and those who report to you. Mike has to answer to his boss to meet his expectations, but how does that affect those employees who answer to Mike and his responsibilities to them? This triadic dilemma is prevalent throughout all industries and must be deliberately addressed. If Mike focuses on keeping his boss satisfied at his employees' cost, he may instill low morale and still not achieve his quotas. On the other hand, if he focuses on his employees at the cost of his relationship with his boss, he may lose his job.

According to balance theory, when three individuals (in this case: the President, CEO, and employee) develop different levels of relational exchange, an imbalance will arise among them that may result in hostile sentiments or poor interaction.[24] When these relationships are out of balance, all three parties suffer. So how does the leader deal with this typically unsettled situation?

Leadership is the answer. Remember the earlier statement—if there is no one to lead, there is no need for leadership. The balancing act for a leader is to convey their boss's demands to their employees, giving them the tools and support they need to be successful, affirmed, and secure in their work. At times, this will mean "running interference"—that is, intervening on their employees' behalf to protect them from distraction or annoyance

---

24 Tse, H., Lawrence, S., Lam, C., & Huang, X. (2013). 'When my supervisor dislikes you more than me: The effect of similarity in leader–member exchange on coworkers' interpersonal emotion and perceived help. *Journal of Applied Psychology*, 98(6), 974–988.

from their boss to ensure that they have the time, tools, and opportunities to succeed.

Takeaway: Running interference for employees does not mean that the leader ignores their boss's needs: it means clearly communicating with the boss so that they are confident that their needs, too, will be met and that the team is working toward that end. This open communication must focus on the clear expectations of all parties involved. I would suggest that the balance point in this triadic relationship is a focus on clear expectations.

Mike returned to his office and sat down to organize an all-hands meeting with his employees. He knew that he needed to highlight the past quarter's successes and address their identified deficiencies. He also knew that he would need to focus on finding suitable replacement leaders for human resources and domestic sales. He clearly realized that, as now CEO, his priority was no longer the problem of not achieving his quotas or losing two directors: it was the urgency to bring out the best in his employees and himself in order to find solutions and grow the business. Mike remembered those who had inspired him to inspire others.

Why we choose to lead must always be kept at the forefront of a leader's mind, which takes us to the final reason why leadership isn't more enjoyable.

Questions to consider:

- Why is communicating the organizational vision important to those whom the leader answers to?

- How could Mike better engage his boss in the next quarter to create confidence and articulate his vision to realize success?

The Elusive *Why* We Lead

We started this book with a discussion on *why* people choose leadership positions and suggested that it was essential to know the *why*. It may seem redundant to readdress that question but, in reality, it is very easy to lose sight of the *why*. Admittedly, I learned the implications of losing focus on the *why* first-hand in my own leadership roles. Human nature is such that we can easily become preoccupied by day-to-day pressures and lose sight of our long-term vision.

Perhaps leaders become complacent in their leadership position because, on their selection, they assume that they have "arrived" and can now call the shots and make big decisions. Instead of recognizing the dynamic and volatile nature of their position and the need to continually seek new opportunities to adjust to it, many leaders incorrectly assume that the environment must adapt to them and that the opportunities will then naturally come their way.[25] They truly believe they have "arrived"!

25 Uhl-Bien, M., & Arena, M. (2018). Leadership for organizational adaptability: A theoretical synthesis and integrative framework. *The Leadership Quarterly*, 29(1), 89–104. doi:10.1016/j.leaqua.2017.12.009

It is often said that life is a journey and, in that context, it may also be appropriate to view leadership as a journey as well. No two people are alike, so—when leading many—what may be effective for one may not be so for others. The dynamic nature of dealing with human beings requires that leaders chart their path with vision and define long-term success for the organization. I remember my first leadership position in the military and how I decided to define success. While my definition may have been a little short-sighted, it did help me keep my focus in check. I measured success by enhancing one person's life in the organization through my leadership.

You might agree that this was short-sighted because it may have caused me to focus on achieving that one success rather than the success of the whole organization. In reality, for me, it was just the opposite. I viewed the organization as a whole and set my sights on taking care of every member of it to the best of my abilities, in line with our mission statement and vision. At the same time, my goal was always to make each person more confident and efficient. Assuming I would likely not know the true impact for years to come, my goal was still to serve each individual to the best of my ability. My leadership *why* was clear and straightforward.

While perhaps a useful and straightforward definition for success, the real question a leader must ask and answer is "How will I measure this success?" If one can't measure it objectively, it becomes subjective and what may be success to one may not be success to another. The key to ensuring success for individuals within an organization is one of expectations. What would the leader expect from the follower regarding growth and performance, and what would the follower expect from the leader regarding opportunity and improvement in work environment?

Determining expectations on both sides requires developing and sustaining a relationship. As we know, relationships take time to develop and sustain, and time is a variable we must all manage. Relationships managed well flourish, while those neglected diminish. If we wish to sustain our reason for leading and commit to measuring success, we must invest time in relationships.

Ironically, the one thing we are all given and have control over is time management. We are given 24 hours every day and it is our choice how we use that time. As leaders, we recognize that we typically have to deal with the problems people face but we do have a choice as to whether we use our time finding new opportunities to benefit the organization or just adding the problems to the other unaddressed ones that are having a negative impact on our time management. We also recognize the importance of looking beyond the immediate to visualize the future success that we aim to achieve.

Takeaway: Creating a vision and adjusting it to a changing environment is a deliberate process. It requires studying the new challenges and the context in which we compete before planning a way forward. We need time to conceptualize our approach and then visualize its success. And, finally, we must a) articulate the vision behind our approach to those in the organization, and b) model and support it each and every day.

Also, leaders must take the time to understand their boss's expectations and ensure that they communicate their progress to both their boss and their employees. Leaders must choose where to focus most of their work time, either on ensuring that their boss is satisfied with their performance or on their employees so that they can understand, meet, or exceed the needs of all parties. How leaders use their time, and why they choose to use it as they do, is directly related to sustaining their reason for leading and whether they find joy in the leadership process.

You see—everything we have discussed so far builds on itself. *Why* we lead and *who* we are helps us to navigate the inherent leadership challenges and avoid the dangers. Dealing with these challenges and dangers equips us to deliberately devote time to exploring why leadership isn't more enjoyable. Now, those leaders willing to pursue finding joy in leadership must dare to be different by taking the time to create a culture of mutual accountability, as we shall see in Part IV.

Questions to consider:

- Why are daily routines, which remind leaders why they chose to lead, important?

- Steven Covey suggests, "Begin each day with the end in mind."[26] How does this translate to ensuring that the *why* doesn't elude the leader?

26 Covey, S. R. (2004). *The 7 habits of highly effective people: Powerful lessons in personal change.* Simon and Schuster.

Part III Recap:
Why Isn't Leadership More Enjoyable?

- To be a successful leader requires perseverance to deal with several fundamentals of human behavior and interaction.
- The inherently complex nature of human beings requires a basic understanding of the need for *affirmation* and *security*, while also acknowledging a human being's innate *selfish desires* to control their domain.
- Leaders must *embrace problems* with a positive attitude, and also encourage ingenuity and innovation in seeking reasons *why* something may not work as a way of figuring out *how* to make it work.
- Leaders must *look beyond the immediate* to the possibilities of the future, trusting in their people and the processes that have brought success in the past.
- The *balancing act for leaders* is to clearly communicate their boss's demands to their employees, giving them the tools and support they need to be successful, affirmed, and secure in their work.
- How leaders use their time, and why they choose to use it as they do, is directly related to *sustaining their reasons* for leading and the extent to which they find joy in the leadership process.

Part IV:

Mutual Accountability:
Dare to be Different

Life is about choices and the natural consequences of those choices. Because choices have consequences, we must assume some accountability for the choices made. But what is accountability? Accountability is "the capacity for holding people answerable for their own decisions and actions which enables the systems and structures of social order to operate".[27] This definition suggests that accountability is necessary for social order and yet—under the umbrella of the COVID-19 global pandemic—our lives have appeared to be anything but orderly.

As mentioned in Part I of this book, the world as we knew it was turned upside down when the global pandemic hit and all but "essential" personnel were told to stay at home as the so-called experts sorted it all out. Unfortunately, as I write this Part IV (well over a year after the pandemic hit the United States), the so-called experts are still sorting it out. Six-foot distancing and wearing a mask are still the norm in most states, and even stricter guidelines persist in many parts of the

27 Hall, R., Frink, D., & Buckley, R. (2017). An accountability account: A review and synthesis of the theoretical and empirical research on felt accountability. *Journal of Organizational Behavior*, 38(2), 204–224. doi:10.1002/job.2052

world. Government authorities have made these rules mandatory with potential repercussions for those who fail to comply. Everyone is expected to be accountable so that the systems and structures of social order will operate effectively.

But what happens when leaders live by a different set of rules and are not accountable to those they lead? Inconsistency or hypocrisy sacrifices the very unity leaders are expected to preserve.[28] Put more bluntly, what followers find intolerable are "empty words masking real power".[29] "Do as I say and not as I do" is a statement of power, not of influence, and one that creates division and crushes unity.

Part II of this book explains how power not only breeds power but also shifts an organization's focus to the selfish sustainment and growth of that power at all costs. This unquenchable thirst for power, which is why we labeled it "a danger," robs a leader of any joy in leading and at the same time destroys morale within the organization. If the hypocrisy of one-way accountability is so dangerous and harmful, there must be another approach that benefits both leader and organization.

Achieving success usually requires navigating the path less traveled, and overcoming challenges and dangers to successfully reach the objective. We have to know *why* we should choose this path and we must have the discipline to complete the journey.

---

28 Bourcier, B. (2019). Rescuing politics from lying and hypocrisy: Utility and truth in Jeremy Bentham's thought. *Ethics, Politics & Society*, Vol. 2.
29 Bourcier, 'Rescuing politics'.

I will now describe the challenging yet rewarding process of creating a culture of mutual accountability for those who dare to be different. But first we must *understand the difference between accountability and mutual accountability,* and we must then *invest in deliberately developing the structures that support a culture of mutual accountability.*

When leaders and followers realize the benefits of this investment and how it can lead to success, the foundation is laid for the process of developing trust that all can count on. This process, which I shall detail in Parts V and VI, is the culmination of everything we have discussed up to now and it significantly relies on the commitment to create a culture of mutual accountability. With the appropriate commitment to make a special effort and master the fundamentals that this culture requires, finding joy in leadership is an attainable goal.

In Part III, I explained that what separated the "Greatest of All Time" athletes from their competitors was mastering the fundamentals of their craft. If we desire to experience the joy of leadership, establishing the foundation for a culture of mutual accountability and the required fundamentals is paramount to success. It is what separates those who thrive as leaders and those who merely survive. Thus, if you dare to find joy in leadership, creating a culture of mutual accountability is the first step in the right direction!

Accountability Versus Mutual Accountability

At the beginning of this Part IV, we defined accountability as holding people answerable for their decisions and actions to support social order within organizations and gatherings but, too often, organizational accountability appears to be one-way. This is immediately evident from a Google Scholar search on mutual accountability compared with accountability: the concept of mutual accountability receives much less attention. Perhaps this is because the concept relies on two-way agreement.

Because of the difficulty in adapting such a concept to local culture and values, and its dependence on a system of shared social norms, recent research suggests that mutual accountability is considered more of an art than a science.[30] As we have already established, a culture of shared social norms is contained within the *why* of an organization and how the members support the organizational *why*. For this discussion, we will refer to Harvard PhD Faaiza Rashid's definition of mutual accountability as an "intimate awareness of the effects of our actions on one another, holding each other accountable for progress and outcomes".[31]

Working with several different special operations units during my military career, I experienced the intimate awareness of the effects of one's actions on other people. Before any mission is executed, the entire plan is

---

30 Phillips, R. (2020). *The Perception of Mutual Accountability within the LMX: Its Influence on the Supervisor and Employee Relationship*. A dissertation presented in partial fulfillment of the requirements for the degree Doctorate of Philosophy, Grand Canyon University, Phoenix, Arizona.

31 Rashid, F. (2015). *Mutual Accountability and its Influence on Team Performance*. Doctoral dissertation, Harvard University, Graduate School of Arts & Sciences. http://nrs.harvard.edu/urn-3:HUL.InstRepos:14226095

choreographed in meticulous detail so that every team member knows what to expect from their teammates. The reason for the mission—the *why*—is transparently communicated, leaving no doubt or confusion. Every member of the team knows their role and takes ownership of that role. This is what they train for every day.

For an organization to keep its *why* at the forefront every day, it relies on mutual accountability through a creed or value charter. This guides the actions of each member of the organization and reminds them of their mutual commitment to the relationship. One such creed is the United States Army's Ranger Creed, which I have summarized below:

Ranger Creed

Recognizing: They volunteered, knowing the *expectations* and accepting responsibility for their choice

Acknowledging: They are a part of something greater than themselves (*relational expectations*)

Never: Giving anything less than their best for their fellow Rangers (*mutual accountability*)

Gallantly: Representing the Ranger Corps in everything they do (*transparency*)

Energetically: Discharging their duties as a Ranger (*ownership*)

Readily: Displaying the courage required to the bitter end (*commitment to the process*)

The massive cargo plane departs the west coast of the United States loaded with paratroopers and equipment to begin the 15-hour mission that will cross the Pacific Ocean, covering over 5,200 miles to reach its objective, and drop the paratroopers precisely on time and on target. After take-off, there is strict radio silence with no transmissions, flying alone across the ocean. The mission includes the intensity of two in-flight air refueling rendezvous.

The heavy-loaded cargo aircraft only has about five hours of fuel when fully loaded, so these two high-intensity air refuelings are needed to reach the target area. Doing all this with perfect timing, extremely close contact between two large aircraft, and no radio transmissions highlights the intimate awareness of one's actions on another. Finally, once the aircraft is over the Korean peninsula, fighter aircraft will escort the cargo plane to the drop zone. Every organization and participant is counting on every individual involved to play their part: if any one component fails, the risk would increase dramatically and the entire mission could be compromised.

Takeaway: Mutual accountability is not a one-time event: it is a continuing process of maintaining full awareness of each other's actions, holding each other accountable, and knowing that they have your full support and you have theirs. It is about the predictability of your actions being strictly in line with the expectations of the relationship. While accountability is about answerability, mutual accountability is about the relationship of answerability that demands co-ownership.

Because mutual accountability is more about developing trust between all parties, it requires time, commitment, and investment beyond that needed in holding another answerable for their actions. Laying a foundation for success, regardless of the size of the organization or the mission, requires a shared commitment to the organization's underlying principles to ensure the integrity of the foundation to support the structure for which it was designed. If we dare to seek the joy of leadership and to develop a culture of mutual accountability within an organization, the investment decisions must be deliberate and in line with the underlying principles of the organization when first created.

Questions to consider:

- Why is the construct of mutual accountability not as widespread in society as the construct of accountability?

- Why would mutual accountability be described as more of an art than a science?

Investment Decisions: Relation or Relationship/ Workplace or Organizational Team Environment

Leaders of an organization will often identify personnel problems as the most significant challenges they face in their day-to-day work. Whether the problem involves firing an employee, hiring a replacement, or dealing with the personalities within the management team, personnel matters routinely come up as stressors for leaders who must continually deal with the conundrum of finding good people to contribute to the team.

In the hiring process, a leader sets the parameters and qualities they require, takes the time to review all candidates, participates in the interviewing process, and makes the final decision. Most times, the hiring process is effective: the right person is selected and they make a significant contribution to the organization. If the hiring process continually fails, a different leader may be needed.

Often the assumption is that, when the right person is hired, they will immediately fit into place and start fixing the problems their predecessor left behind. This is rarely the case, suggesting that it is not only hiring the right person but also developing them that is most important. And, if development is the key, then who should be responsible for it?

When a professional athlete is acquired by a new team, it is the team's leaders who have assessed whether the person will fit in and help the team succeed in the future. Once hired, the athlete is immediately

94

immersed in the new system and the new team culture. Assistant coaches will act as mentors to further develop the induction process and give support throughout the season.

The typical industry experience is the same: even for the initial 90 days when a new employee is indoctrinated in the organization's administrative fundamentals: payroll, human resources, initial training, formal mission, vision, and guiding principles. Once this orientation is complete, the new hire is given a supervisor who may or may not commit to their further development. This is the stage when you can examine whether the new employee was the right choice and whether the leader is investing in the process of continual development intended to permeate throughout the organization.

Two critical investment decisions need to be made by leaders committed to creating a culture of mutual accountability. First, whether they will invest in relations or relationships and, second, whether they will create an ordinary workplace or a more sophisticated organizational team environment where communications and expectations are transparently and consistently articulated. Each of these decisions renders different results.

Relation or Relationship?

Websites like Ancestry.com and 23andMe.com have earned success by giving people a means to learn more about their ancestry and to connect with long-lost or newly discovered relatives. Having done this myself, I was astonished to find out that I had over 1,400 DNA relatives. In the context of this discussion, I was related to over 1,400 people and I only knew of about 10! In fact, over my nearly four decades in the workplace, I had certainly made acquaintance with almost as many people whom I probably knew much better than my DNA relatives.

Acknowledging an association does not suggest any knowledge, understanding, or even the slightest bit of accountability within it. In a 2015 study on performance and accountability relations in a large welfare administration reform in Norway, researchers found that "as an organization reforms, accountability within that organization becomes ambiguous and contested, suggesting accountability within an organization is both dynamic and conditional".[32] Without a relationship in which expectations are transparently communicated, accountability atrophies and becomes lost in the process.

Going back to our story in Part I about the small business owner who restructured the company to make some *real money*, the shift in focus from people to revenue changed the organization's accountability relationship. Employees and customers no longer felt that they were part of an integrity-focused team because of the owner's move away from his original vision—one that had brought them all together in the first place. Thus, the small business became just another paycheck

32 Phillips, *Perception of Mutual Accountability.*

to its employees and many of the customers looked to partner elsewhere. Because accountability is both dynamic and conditional, leaders who wish to create a culture of mutual accountability must constantly invest in and foster relationships.

Early on, I was fortunate to have a mentor guide me with a model of mutual accountability, all through leading by example. What was so noteworthy about this leader was his sincere interest in my personal and professional growth. When we were in discussion, it seemed as if there was nothing more important to him than what we were talking about and, even more so, what my thoughts were. I have never met a better listener or communicator. He was a true leader who lived by the concept of mutual accountability.

Takeaway: When a leader invests in a relationship with a follower, transparent communications and relational expectations become by-products. Because I knew that this mentor had my best interests in mind, I took careful note of our conversations and candidly shared my thoughts. When my mentor suggested an expectation, I knew this would be something good for me to achieve and, in most cases, I had already observed my mentor exhibiting the same behavior.

Actions speak louder than words, so this leader's expectations seldom had to be articulated. Realizing the impact this investment had had on me, I was inspired to model the same behavior to others. Throughout my entire 23-year military career, my mentor was consistently engaged in my personal and professional growth through his transparent communications, relational expectations, and empowerment, continually modeling a mutually accountable relationship. My own investment in this relationship had an impact on all my various career roles and my personal family life. The point of sharing this example is to highlight the importance of investing in others. Doing so not only has a significant impact on those within a mutually accountable relationship but also extends beyond the relationship into the communities where these people live and work. When mutually accountable members gather, because of the solid foundation that has been laid, they are now able to have an impact on their work environment.

Questions to consider:

- Why should there be a limit to the number of relationships a leader can invest in?

- Investments are never grounded in perfectly accurate information and thus some fail. Why is it still worth investing in relationships at work?

Workplace or Organizational Team Environment?

From all indications to date, the COVID-19 pandemic may have permanently changed the concept of the workplace. When the country went into lockdown and only essential workers were physically allowed in their workplace, businesses worldwide started working virtually from home. As we slowly start heading back to some form of normalcy, many organizations are considering maintaining many of their employees in a virtual capacity environment.

This new virtual workplace environment has led to many people relocating from the cities into the suburbs or across the country, avoiding the high costs of living, commuting, and other associated challenges. Despite the pandemic restrictions, this approach appears to work for many organizations and it suggests a potential norm for the future.

While technology and innovation create the means to have these new workspaces, the impact this virtual norm will have on human behavior, leadership effectiveness, and organizational effectiveness remains uncertain. A study completed by a team at Manchester University focused on the consequences of various communication methods for leading virtual teams and found that cohesive work was often hindered by "differing, and often competing priorities and objectives between the members".[33] Therefore, this new virtual landscape requires leadership engagement and employee investment to ensure that all parties are in agreement, synchronized to achieve desired goals and objectives.

Anyone who has worked from home will confess that it takes much discipline to stay focused and not be distracted by competing domestic interests. Leadership

---

33 Morgan, L., Paucar-Caceres, A., & Wright, G. (2014). Leading effective global virtual teams: The consequences of methods of communication. *Systemic Practice and Action Research*, 27(6), 607–624.

in this work structure requires a consistent approach involving transparent communications with deliberate clarification of goals and objectives by both leaders and team members.[34] Within this virtual environment, all typical leadership approaches in the workplace must be adaptable to facilitate an organizational team environment whereby two-way communication and relational expectations are the norms.

An emergency call comes in from McMurdo Station, Antarctica, requesting an immediate rescue mission to recover a team member who has suffered a severe heart attack. An experienced crew is tasked to fly out of Christchurch, New Zealand, on this life-saving mission that will require seamless communications and co-ordination with team members from California, Hawaii, New Zealand, and Antarctica.

The secure teleconference of this multi-location team begins with the mission leader stating the mission objective and emphasizing the critical need for every team member to transparently communicate their daily status, concerns, and issues. He knows that these are critical to the mission's success. The leader then focuses on the anticipated challenges lying ahead and how to overcome them as a team. He finishes his brief by making it clear to every team member that his

---

34 Morgan et al., 'Leading effective global virtual teams'.

job, as he viewed it, was to ensure that everyone on the team had the information and tools they needed for success.

Takeaway: The workplace of the past, where the organization's culture was often defined by the members present within the physical workspace, is being replaced with a virtual and more dynamic workplace whereby communications and expectations must be transparently and consistently articulated. Assumptions of the past must be replaced with new actions by leaders to ensure that the team goals are clear and to emphasize the need for two-way feedback. The leadership commitment to an organizational team environment, combined with a sincere investment in mutually accountable team member relationships, provides the structure needed to establish a culture of mutual accountability. Once this structure is established, the leadership is ready to lay the cultural foundation of transparency, predictability, and growth.

Questions to consider:

- What are the obstacles to creating a team-centric organization in a virtual setting?

- What is gained or lost from using virtual interaction tools compared with in-person face-to-face interactions?

Laying the Cultural Foundation: Transparency, Predictability, and Growth

Daring to be different by choosing to create a culture of mutual accountability requires more time, greater commitment, and total investment by leaders. Their time, commitment, and investment are focused on the people they choose to lead and retaining those people is at the forefront of the cultural development process. The September 2016 issue of the *Harvard Business Review* pointed out that people generally leave their jobs because of leadership issues, limited opportunity for growth or promotion, or an offer of a better opportunity elsewhere.[35]

Retaining good employees is the desire of every employer in order to mitigate recruiting and replacement costs, and the likely effects of these on long-term organizational cohesion. What makes retention even more challenging is the human tendency to compare oneself with a friend who may or may not be in a better situation in another organization. This phenomenon is made more prominent in today's social media environment, which ensures that news of other people apparently in a more favorable situation than you—although they may not be—is widely publicized.

Determining the factors for retaining good employees is a driving force behind an organization's long-term success. In a study on the leader–employee relationship and its impact on employee commitment,

---

35 Garland, P. (2016, September). Why people quit their jobs. *Harvard Business Review*. https://hbr.org/2016/09/why-people-quit-their-jobs

four factors were found to be significant to retaining employees: affect, contribution, loyalty, and professional respect.[36] It is clear: employees want to feel respected in an organization where they believe they are making a difference both personally and professionally, but they also desire a work environment built on trust. When members of an organization feel that they are a part of something meaningful and bigger than themselves, they are ready for the leadership to lay the foundation for mutual accountability.

The Antarctic rescue team completed their teleconference: all members appeared satisfied that the identified risks could be mitigated, and they were all in sync in terms of execution, goals, and objectives. The aircraft launched from the west coast the following morning to pre-position in Hawaii with flight plans to continue to Christchurch the next day.

The assumption that all the rescue team members were in agreement regarding contribution, trust, and respect went further to include a shared understanding of knowing the advantage of openness throughout the team in implementing the risk mitigation strategies effectively. Unfortunately, we discovered later that not

36 Miller, L. (2018). *Leader-Employer Relationship as an Antecedent to Employee Commitment Mediating Innovative Work Behavior*. A dissertation presented in partial fulfillment of the requirements for the degree Doctorate of Business Administration, Capella University, Atlanta, Georgia.

all team members were fully transparent in their lack of shared understanding and instead aired their concerns independently after the team had departed. Specifically, they were unable to appreciate the crew's experience, unique qualifications, and the timeliness of this mission for both the patient and the Antarctic conditions. Sun Tzu, the foremost expert on military operations, commented on this behavior by pointing out that "those unable to understand the dangers inherent in employing troops are equally unable to understand the advantageous ways of doing so".[37]

The lack of transparency in communicating concerns about the off-season risks (weather, daylight, and temperature) early on delayed the departure of the rescue mission from Hawaii for days. By the time the concerns were addressed so that the mission could move on to New Zealand, the rescue mission had turned into a recovery mission. The aircraft did make its way to McMurdo despite the challenges associated with an off-season mission but, instead of rescuing a patient for medical attention, they carried out a body for burial.

Understanding the advantages of employing followers committed to something bigger than themselves requires

37 Griffith, S. (1971). *Sun Tzu: The art of war.* Oxford University Press.

leaders whose words, actions, and empowerment are constantly provided for followers to rely on. *Laying a solid foundation for a culture of mutual accountability requires transparency, predictability, and growth.*

Transparency

We began this journey together with a discussion of why people seek leadership positions. Knowing our role, talents, and contributions is directly tied to finding joy in the workplace. As important as it is to know who you are and why you are where you are, being true to yourself and displaying your authentic and uncensored self to others is what relational transparency is all about.[38]

Transparency is often referred to as "authenticity," and this is paramount to laying a foundation for a mutually accountable culture—there is no room for façades or pretense. When you invest in a relationship with another person, you want to know that you are steadily learning more about each other and not dealing with a different personality each time you engage.

The frustrations many of us feel with politics today is how a politician's position can be the complete opposite of what they stood for a month ago. No one is ever accountable if they are inconsistent in what they stand for. Transparency requires an uncensored reflection of who you are and what you represent. Certainly, positions can change based on new information and circumstances but, within a transparent relationship, these changes are easily explained without compromising our true selves.

---

38 Waite, R., McKinney, M., Smith-Glasgow, M., & Meloy, F. (2014). The embodiment of authentic leadership. *Journal of Professional Nursing*, 30(4), 282–291.

Assumptions are often based on the perceptions of a given situation or circumstance. As discussed earlier, in special operations units, it is assumed that teammates within the organization will look out for and help each other. This is based on the expectation that each team member is transparent in their unwavering support for each other. This type of environment was described in an article on leadership influences on team performance in which the researchers stated that transparency "involves making personal disclosures, such as openly sharing information and expressing true thoughts and feelings".[39]

Transparency is a fluid process that invites ongoing communication and feedback—saying what you mean, meaning what you say, and being willing to accept feedback from those around you who are doing the same. The candor and collaboration involved in this process build a team environment that all team members can count on. But, because of the risks associated with transparency, many are unwilling to follow this path unless leaders demonstrate the behavior first and show that it is safe to operate in a transparent environment.

So what is transparency or a transparent relationship? First, transparency is disclosing information directly relevant to an issue. For example, when asked about the risks associated with an off-season landing in Antarctica, it would be inappropriate to suggest that the patient's weight could be associated with cardiac issues.

39 Lyubovnikova, L., Legood, N., Turner, N., & Mamakouka, A. (2017). How authentic leadership influences team performance: The mediating role of team reflexivity. *Journal of Business Ethics*, 141(1), 59–70.

While there may be several important factors related to the patient's health, they are extraneous to discussing the risks involved in landing on ice.

Second, transparency is full disclosure as relevant to the context. When a crew member was asked about previous off-season landings on the ice, a response that cited the fact that there had been no accidents within the past 10 years, but omitted to say that there was an accident 11 years ago, would not be transparent.

Third, transparency is being honest and speaking out. In the multi-party teleconference, the discussion included risk factors and risk mitigation. When one team member had concerns that they failed to voice for fear of going against the consensus, their silence by omission conflicted with transparency.

Takeaway: In the spirit of transparency, even though we may not understand a discussion's intricacies, it is one's responsibility to air one's genuine thoughts and feelings. It may just be intuition but, if something just doesn't feel right, it is always worth raising it within the group for everyone collectively to either figure it out or determine that it is irrelevant. When members of an organization can communicate transparently, make appropriate disclosures, openly share information, and express true thoughts and feelings, the seeds are planted for a mutually accountable environment. Not only will the team members be able to count on each other but a sense of confidence or predictability will also grow within the team.

Questions to consider:

- Why is it difficult for members of a team to express their true thoughts?

- What principles guide the discussion in a transparent conversation?

Predictability

Human beings are curious creatures constantly striving to make sense of their world and their purpose. As we learn more about our environment and ourselves, we gain in understanding and begin to make sense of it. At a young age, we learn about gravity and believe that what goes up must come down. Scholars from the distant past have been discovering laws and theories to help us better understand the world around us and predict outcomes based upon them.

Predicting outcomes is a lifelong quest from a baby's cry to be fed to the realization that we won't live forever. We believe that, through such predictions, we maintain more control over our future lives and experience a sense of harmony in the present. In the workplace, we try and predict job satisfaction, support, and exchange from our leaders, and a commitment from the organization to act on its promises.[40]

The terms an employee expects to be upheld are those of their employment contract: pay, hours, vacation, responsibilities, and support from their

40 Nichols, A., & Cottrell, C. (2014). What do people desire in their leaders? The role of leadership level on trait desirability. *Leadership Quarterly*, 25(4), 711–729.

supervisor. The leader/supervisor expects the employee to uphold their part of the employment contract and the expectations outlined in their job description. It all seems straightforward and yet the future for most employees is anything but predictable.

The *2019 Retention Report* from the Work Institute suggested that 27% of employees voluntarily left their jobs in 2018 and predicted that, if this trend continued, it would be 35% by 2023![41] Every preventable category highlighted that employees realized less than their predicted expectations: career development, work–life balance, manager behavior, compensation, well-being, job characteristics, and work environment.[42] The costs alone of rehiring and retraining 27% of the workforce points to the need for a better approach to retaining employees.

While statistics help us to predict how many employees leave organizations and why, perhaps we need to understand what predictability is and how it has an impact on both leaders and followers. Predictability is a belief based on past performance and behaviors: we can predict with some certainty that another will behave in a particular manner.[43] In other words, the behaviors and actions we experience in the past create expectations for predicting how someone might behave and act in the future.

41 Mahan, T., Nelms, D., Bearden, C., & Pearce, B. (2019). 2019 *Retention report*. Work Institute. https://info.workinstitute.com/hubfs/2019%20Retention%20Report/Work%20Institute%20 2019%20Retention%20Report%20final-1.pdf
42 Mahan et al., 2019 Retention report, pp. 4–7.
43 Phillips, *Perception of Mutual Accountability.*

Takeaway: Consistency in actions and behaviors supports predictability and inconsistency enhances unpredictability. In 2018, unpredictability created feelings of unmet expectations, leading 27% of employees to look for employment elsewhere.[44] So creating predictability within the workplace is fiscally sound, and may decrease turnover and increase productivity. Within the context of creating a mutually accountable culture, this is achieved through relational expectations.

The last time we visited the concept of relational expectations in depth was in Part II. We discussed it as an inherent challenge associated with leadership and, clearly, it *is* a challenge. We discussed the continual effort of seeking relational expectations on both sides to ensure clear understanding and trust. When we fully understand the circumstances and situation we're in, we can predict, with some certainty, the outcome.

This understanding comes from our own experiences and those of others. It is through this understanding that predictability and trust evolve. This was best illustrated by the miracle on the Hudson (described in Part II), where the entire team safely executed a monumental task with little to no guidance or time. The culture of mutual accountability created by Captain Sullenberger's transparent communications and clearly understood relational expectations led to a task that was—predictably—flawlessly executed in minutes and saved the lives of all involved. Through these real-life

44 Mahan et al., 2019 *Retention report.*

stories, we can enhance our intuition based on experience and knowledge, paving the way for the final key ingredient to creating a mutually accountable culture: personal and professional growth.

Questions to consider:

- How are expectations and predictability tied together?

- How does our need for affirmation and security have an impact on the importance of predictability?

Personal and Professional Growth

Remember our millennial Mark in Part II? He had only been in the organization for nine months and was already looking for a promotion. The millennial generation is not only looking for promotion opportunities: in many cases, they expect them. It is not uncommon for a millennial to leave a job without another opportunity just because they feel that they are stagnating in their current position and have no prospects looming on the horizon.

Personal and professional growth was also listed in Part II as a challenge for leaders, and the *2019 Retention Report* suggests that it remains a challenge for retaining employees.[45] While it is suggested that the millennial generation is more focused on promotion opportunities than past generations, the reality is that most, if not all, employees want the chance to grow personally and

---

45 Mahan et al., 2019 Retention report, p.13.

professionally. According to regulatory focus theory, people wish to avoid pain and enjoy pleasure in their day-to-day lives.[46] As we discussed in the Introduction, we long for the *motivational salience* of being promoted or receiving an award.

As biological creatures, we seek the pleasures of dopamine, serotonin, and oxytocin in our day-to-day activities, and we navigate to activities within our lives that provide these responses. Creating a mutually accountable culture requires leaders and followers to look for growth opportunities and articulate the possibilities to each other. Employees, at all levels, want to do their best and to continue learning and developing.[47] In fact, they are often hired for this reason.

If an employee is hired based on their growth potential—and takes the job based on the same—where is the breakdown in the process? In the movie *Field of Dreams* produced by Kevin Costner, an Iowa corn farmer hears a voice one night in his cornfield telling him to build a baseball diamond. The voice suggests that, if he does, some of the great players of the past will come to his ballpark and play. Crazy as it may seem, leadership visions and pursuit of opportunities produce results. Employees and leaders alike need to articulate their dreams and believe that they can come true.

Early in my military career, I was introduced to the "3×5 card Five-Year Plan." I would take a 3×5 index

46 Tuncdogan, A., Acar, O., & Stam, D. (2017). Individual differences as antecedents of leader behavior: Towards an understanding of multi-level outcomes. *The Leadership Quarterly*, 28(1), 40–64. doi:10.1016/j.leaqua2016.10.011
47 Phillips, *Perception of Mutual Accountability.*

card, draw a horizontal line through the middle of it, and then section the line off into five one-year sections. Beginning with the current year, I would assign each section to a consecutive year until the card depicted a view of the next five years. Then, within each of these year sections, I would write down my goals and aspirations.

The card forced me to continually look ahead, keeping my goals and aspirations in mind. In hindsight, I will tell you that 85% or greater of what was written on those cards came to fruition. "If you build it, they will come" can be as simple as a 3×5 index card! What is important here is conceiving the dream, writing it down, and then referring to it regularly. Personal and professional growth goals need to be frequently discussed and evaluated. The ownership of the written goals is the author's, but leaders need to be aware of them, facilitate opportunities for the person's success, and provide feedback along the way.

Personal and professional growth suggests an expectation of feedback and improvement. Unfortunately, in many organizations, feedback is commonly neglected or considered an afterthought among leaders. Leaders and supervisors often feel forced to accomplish annual feedback sessions, especially because the human resources department has a mandate to ensure that they are completed on time. Unfortunately, this attitude leaves many leaders viewing feedback as a *necessary evil* instead of a critically helpful tool for achieving results.

Takeaway: Throughout my professional career, I consistently found that my colleagues and fellow workers longed for feedback. We spend most of our formative years receiving feedback from our parents, teachers, coaches, and friends. Then, once we enter the workplace, most of us experience a void in the feedback process other than the formal feedback we receive during our annual performance appraisal. Without frequent feedback, complacency replaces initiative and growth is stunted.

The catalysts for creating a mutually accountable culture are transparency, predictability, and growth. Each of these action words requires a continuous commitment to the relationship, just as a garden needs continuous attention to yield the desired results. Like a garden, if a relationship is neglected for too long, the amount of work necessary to return it to its earlier fruitful stage is immense. On the other hand, if tended to appropriately, it can be a *labor of love* bringing joy to the day.

Accountability and mutual accountability are two different constructs. One is the capacity for holding people answerable for their own decisions and actions, and the other is an intimate awareness of the effects of our actions on one another, holding each other accountable for progress and outcomes. One is relatively passive, while the other is active. Leaders who wish to find joy in leadership must dare to be different from those who just want to survive the experience. Building a culture of mutual accountability can take a lot of work initially. Still, the investment bears fruit that is priceless within the organization, as we shall see in Parts V and VI, "Developing Trust You Can Count On," by discovering

Why trust matters, *How* trust has an impact on the organization, *What* trust does for the relationship and *Who* we become.

Questions to consider:

- Why is it important for human beings to continually learn and grow?

- How have goals and aspirations had an impact on your work and personal life?

Part IV Recap:
Mutual Accountability: *Dare to Be Different*

Accountability versus Mutual Accountability
- *Accountability* is the capacity for holding people answerable for their own decisions and actions, which enables the systems and structures of social order to operate.
- *Mutual accountability* is a continuing process of maintaining an intimate awareness of the relationship's actions, holding each other accountable, and knowing that they have your full support and you have theirs.

Investment Decisions: Relation or Relationship/ Workplace or Organizational Team Environment
- When a leader invests in a *mutually accountable relationship* with a follower, transparent communications and relational expectations become by-products of the relationship.
- The workplace of the past, where the organization's culture was often defined by the members present within the physical workspace, is replaced with a virtual and more *dynamic workplace* where communications and expectations must be transparently and consistently articulated to ensure that all members of the organization are in agreement.
- The leadership investment in an *organizational team environment,* combined with a sincere investment in the *relationship* with team members, opens the door for establishing a culture of mutual accountability.

Laying the Cultural Foundation: Transparency, Predictability, and Growth

- As important as it is to know who you are and why you are where you are, being true to yourself and displaying your authentic and uncensored self to others is what relational transparency is all about.
- Consistencies in actions and behaviors support predictability, and inconsistencies enhance unpredictability.
- Personal and professional growth suggests an expectation of feedback and improvement.
- The catalysts for creating a mutually accountable culture are transparency, predictability, and growth. Without frequent feedback, complacency replaces initiative and growth is stunted.

Part V:

Developing Trust You Can Count On

The Why and The How

I spoke with a friend of mine about playing Division I basketball for Michigan State back in the late 1980s. He was a standout in his high school team and eagerly recruited by Michigan State. I asked him what it was like playing at that level and his reply described what many leaders discover when they reach the next level—everyone is talented and a standout from their previous team. Players and leaders who believe they have arrived and are at the top of their game when they reach the next level need to realize that there is only one direction for them to proceed—downhill!

Those labeled "Greatest of All Time" never believe they have arrived and remain forever committed to improving their profession's fundamentals and finer points. We referred to Tiger Woods in Part III, highlighting how he had changed his already near-perfect swing in his quest for total perfection. Tiger has actually altered his swing four different times. I suspect that, if we asked him why, he would say there is always room for improvement.

You might suggest that perfecting the fundamentals and finer points in any arena of life is a never-ending quest to master the basics. Perhaps we describe medical doctors as *practicing* their profession because the complexities and intricacies of the human body have yet to be mastered, let alone perfected. In that light, we would expect all physicians to continuously seek to improve their knowledge and skills, especially if we require their expertise. Doctors and surgeons renowned in their professions are always looking for innovation and new ways to enhance their skills and knowledge. These practitioners earn the admiration and trust of those within and outside their professions.

Like surgeons, leaders also deal with complex and intricate human beings. They don't remove tumors or replace heart valves but they nevertheless have an impact on their followers' physical and psychological well-being. Leaders renowned for their impact on their followers also earn trust and admiration within their sphere of influence. They are often considered innovators, continually seeking new ways to take care of their followers and bring out the best in them.

With earned trust, both leader and follower engage and interact more effectively, and the health and well-being of their relationship and the organization as a whole are enhanced. By taking the time to develop relationships of trust, leaders create an environment that encourages the continued pursuit of excellence. The challenge in most organizations is whether the leaders will take the time to determine their *trust status* and how they will go about further developing that trust.

We will now assess a proven method for creating trust that leaders can count on. Within the trust developed by creating a culture of mutual accountability, leaders and followers can understand *why* trust matters, *how* it has an impact on an organization, *what* it does for a relationship, and *who* one can become in a trusting environment. By mastering the four fundamentals we have already discussed—transparent communications, relational expectations, personal and professional growth, and ownership, all within the context of mutual accountability—leaders *can* and *will* find joy in leadership.

Encouraging Transparent Communications: *Why* Trust Matters

The phrase, "Say what you mean and mean what you say," has probably never been more challenged than during the COVID-19 pandemic. Throughout the United States, leaders at nearly every level wavered on issues like social distancing, mask-wearing, public transportation, and the deadliness of the virus. The inconsistencies in communications from our leaders and the media significantly diminished trust and polarized the states' views on our respective governments' handling of the pandemic.

When our lives and livelihoods are at stake, trust is a paramount issue most often evaluated by comparing the consistency of someone's actions with their words.

Today's focus on being politically correct, regardless of our personal views, clouds our true intentions while having a negative impact on the trust and well-being of those within our influence. Often, over-generalizations occur when, for an unsubstantiated problem, we evaluate the circumstances through politically correct lenses and generate false assumptions that may have a negative impact on an entire organization or population. For example, throughout much of the COVID-19 pandemic, the lines between the politically motivated and the scientific guidance have been blurred, if not indistinguishable.

When employees believe that decisions are motivated by organizational politics and not the *why* of the organization—namely, trust—this belief has a negative impact on personal well-being. A recent study on the effects of the perception of organizational politics on employee well-being conclusively found that organizational politics had a negative impact on employee well-being and organizational success in the marketplace.[48] Furthermore, the only effective way to lessen this impact was for the leaders to build trust with their employees because, when employees trust their leaders and the organization, their perception of the power of organizational politics is diminished.[49]

Remember the trust issues we discussed between David and Mary in Part II? (David went around the

48 Ullah, S., Hasnain, S. A., Khalid, A., Aslam, A., & Zealand, N. (2019). Effects of perception of organizational politics on employees' well-being: The mediating role of trust and interpersonal conflicts. *European Online Journal of Natural and Social Sciences*, 8(1), 1–14.
49 Ullah et al., 'Effects of perception.'

organization, having closed-door sessions with the other employees complaining about other team members, the management, and the leadership.) Despite having been in the organization for only a short time, David did not trust those around him and he needed to assess the environment himself. Ironically, his inherent lack of trust in others led to others lacking trust in him! Unfortunately, David's story is not uncommon and highlights how organizational trust and, even more, leadership trust within an organization are of real importance within the work environment.

David's story also reveals the insidious nature of a lack of trust within an organization. Without proper attention, this can begin to spread from one individual to another, eventually having an ill effect on the entire organization. We know that an organization's efficiency and effectiveness depend on trust within it. When this is compromised, employees focus on survival at the cost of creativity and ingenuity.

A close friend of mine shared a story about two senior leaders he had previously served under—one fully trusting and the other not so trusting. The not so trusting leader constantly micromanaged the staff, asking for updates on projects and often changing direction before any progress could be made. This leader's approach was to make sure that everything was done to their standards every step of the way, believing that nothing could be done without their direct supervision. This micromanaging approach completely stifled creativity, ingenuity, and progress, robbing staff of initiative and satisfaction. Any prior proactivity shifted to reactivity, just to survive the heavy-handed micromanagement from above.

On the other hand, the fully trusting leader acknowledged upfront that he couldn't do it all and, furthermore, counted on the creativity and ingenuity of those within the organization. He went so far as to direct his employees to "always tell me what you are thinking and, if you have to, force me to listen". This approach encouraged transparent communications and it highlights three reasons *why* trust matters: clarity for decision-making, purpose versus agenda, and respect for the exchange.

Clarity for Decision-making

Sir Ernest Henry Shackleton is renowned as an Irish Antarctic explorer who led three expeditions to the Antarctic. Perhaps his most notable journey was his last on a ship called *Endurance*: the ship became trapped in the ice for 10 months before sinking and yet every member of the expedition survived. Much has been written and documented on this final voyage and I would encourage all leadership scholars to learn more about this incredible story.

When Shackleton advertised for men to join him on the *Endurance* trip, his communication was incredibly transparent:

Men Wanted
for hazardous journey, small wages, bitter cold, long months of complete darkness, constant danger.

> Safe return doubtful, honor and recognition in
> event of success.
> Ernest Shackleton

From start to finish, Shackleton held nothing back. He was careful about what he said, why he said it, and the purpose behind his communications. All his communications and interactions were rooted in his purpose as a leader. He clearly knew *why* he was in this leadership position and the importance of clarity for decision-making.

As a junior officer in the military, I remember a mentor's views on ethical decision-makers. He said that there was no such thing as a bad decision for ethical decision-makers, only bad information. Assuming that ethical decision-makers seek to gather as much information as possible, and assuming that the information they collect is complete and accurate, their decisions are the best they can make based on the information that they have at the time.

Of course, the decision-making process takes into account experience, evaluation, and context. Yet, the above view highlights the importance of a) compiling enough information with which to make an informed decision, and b) checking the clarity and accuracy of that information. Research describes decision-making as a complex, socially interactive, genuine negotiation process that requires being mindful of one's actions and others' reactions.[50] It sounds a little like our definition of mutual accountability, doesn't it?

50 Marchiondo, L., Myers, C., & Kopleman, S. (2015). The relational nature of leadership identity construction: How and when it influences perceived leadership and decision-making. *The Leadership Quarterly*, 26(5), 892–908.

The need for clarity of information for decision-making is relevant here in highlighting the importance of two-way interaction between a leader and their follower in a negotiation process. This ensures a clear understanding of the problem, its context, and possible solutions. As you might imagine, any negotiation's success relies on the good faith of all parties involved. For the reasons suggested in Part IV, this good faith is much more likely to be achieved within a mutually accountable culture.

Mutual accountability provides clarity for leaders and followers. Individuals are more inclined to collaborate with others they perceive to be accountable, and also to trust the decision-making motives of leaders they consider accountable.[51] Throughout an organization, those you believe to be accountable for their actions are those you trust and with whom you feel comfortable negotiating the tough issues.

When Shackleton solicited volunteers through his bold advertisement, he clearly identified what he was looking for as well as what volunteers were to expect. Those selected were accountable for what they signed up for, and they could assume that their leader was similarly accountable, perhaps even more so. They believed that Shackleton would take care of them to the best of his ability throughout the expedition in his expectation of its success.

51 Phillips, R. (2020). *The Perception of Mutual Accountability within the LMX: Its Influence on the Supervisor and Employee Relationship*. A dissertation presented in partial fulfillment of the requirements for the degree Doctorate of Philosophy, Grand Canyon University, Phoenix, Arizona.

Leaders are typically visionary with lofty plans to achieve new levels of excellence and to advance their purpose or cause. Vision can create a roadmap for progress and success but it doesn't have a heartbeat and often relies on those who do in order to achieve the desired outcome. Shackleton had a vision of reaching the South Pole with his selected group, but that vision was secondary to his accountability for taking care of the men who volunteered to undertake the adventure.

Takeaway: Leaders who understand mutual accountability know that their responsibility is to lead those entrusted to them—those who are, in turn, accountable to their leader, having given their support to the leader's vision. Clarity for decision-making requires that the leader knows *why* they lead and to *whom* they are accountable in their leadership. Perhaps Shackleton's most significant accomplishment wasn't exploration but leadership because he demonstrated remarkable accountability to those he led, never losing focus on those who had chosen to follow him.

My military mentor may have been only partially correct about decision-makers. Besides ensuring that they have adequate information with which to make the best decisions, leaders need clarity in their role as decision-makers. In other words, they not only need clarity for decision-making, they also need to clearly understand the personal motivation underlying their leadership role. Encouraging transparency for leaders also requires them to distinguish between purpose and agenda.

Questions to consider:

- If real leadership is about leading those entrusted to one, what obligations do followers have to their leaders regarding the clarity and accuracy of information they provide?

- When an organization is unclear about a leader's guidance, or whether that guidance is conflicting with previous guidance, what kind of impact does that have on transparency and trust?

Purpose Versus Agenda

When the COVID-19 pandemic spread from China to the United States, many so-called experts predicted the possibility of over two million deaths as a result. Their data-driven science models pointed to the cataclysmic effect we might all endure if their predicted overrun of available hospital capacities would quickly be a reality. Decisions were swiftly made to close off flights from China, then other locations overseas, followed by the tremendously damaging decision to shut down the economy to flatten the curve of those becoming infected. The purpose of this decision was clear: we needed to do everything possible to minimize exposure to the virus so that hospital capacity to treat pandemic patients was not overrun.

As time went on and the curve began to flatten, the agendas that different states had pursued in handling the pandemic began to emerge. People in more rural areas started going about their day-to-day activities with respectful caution. By contrast, those in states with more city populations and busy urban communities, seemed more vigilant and—quite frankly—less consistent in their approach to return to work and open up their businesses. It became clear that the varying ideological views of given states led to different approaches for dealing with the pandemic. These inconsistencies highlighted the challenges leaders faced in dealing with the same problem with different agendas not necessarily the most effective for the people under their jurisdiction.

While problem statements and objectives are typically made public in dealing with a crisis, leadership agendas associated with these are not routinely revealed. Leaders often assign tasks without fully outlining the overall plan for success. At the same time, they may have hidden agendas that they are not willing to reveal. In the case of the COVID-19 pandemic, it was speculated that hidden political agendas were having an impact on reopening decisions that then led to inconsistencies between states in terms of decision-making.

As stated earlier, when people believe that decisions are motivated by political considerations, trust within an organization suffers and its efficiency and effectiveness are compromised.[52] This is precisely what the people of the United States felt six months into the pandemic. Trust among the so-called experts was routinely questioned and suggested guidelines, such as

---

52 Ullah et al., 'Effects of perception'.

social distancing and mask-wearing, were inconsistently applied. The public acknowledged the seriousness of the virus but openly questioned the agendas of those advising on the best approach to deal with it.

Encouraging transparency within a mutually accountable culture demands clarity of both purpose and agenda among leaders and followers. Without developing clear plans with transparent agendas to achieve objectives or purposes, competing plans or agendas can undermine both leadership effectiveness and organizational success. Leaders must overtly explain their agendas to their followers, and encourage comment and challenge from them. When agendas are transparent, all involved are clear as to their purpose and the plans to achieve it. When they are not, members typically lose focus and begin to speculate on the sincerity and competence of the leader.

When the *Endurance* was trapped in the Antarctic ice for 10 months, Shackleton kept his crew focused on the day-to-day tasks, assigning duties to all to keep the ship intact until the ice broke and they could continue their journey. His agenda was clear: preserve the crew and the ship. As time went on, there was speculation as to whether the journey would be able to continue or whether it would require a rescue mission. Throughout all these changes, Shackleton was upfront in his intentions to keep the crew intact and to return everyone home safely. The transparency in his purpose and agenda was a crucial factor in keeping everyone alive.

Transparency requires courage from all members of a unit or organization—but especially from those responsible for leadership because, of necessity, they are vulnerable. Vulnerability includes admitting that you do not have all the answers and not all your ideas will be right, so a leader has to count on their team members' input if the agreed plan is to succeed. Ironically, being vulnerable is not new to anyone: leaders who accept vulnerability often return to memories of their early schooldays when learning and growing came with the easy acceptance of knowing that we needed to rely on others.

A 2017 study of the entanglement of leader character and leader competence found that, because both these develop over time, a fundamental transformation occurs when a leader moves beyond a learning orientation and embraces a level of vulnerability, emotional risk, and exposure.[53] One impressive leader I had the pleasure of serving demonstrated those characteristics by overtly spending time with followers whom most would never recognize or who often felt invisible to those above them. This behavior reflects the old aphorism directing people to be as kind to the Janitor as they are to the General.

Transparent communication from a purpose versus agenda perspective demands that leaders make themselves 'visible' and their authority recognized. This means a leader:

- being readily available to those who would not normally have direct access to them;

53 Sturm, R. E., Vera, D., & Crossan, M. (2017). The entanglement of leader character and leader competence and its impact on performance. *The Leadership Quarterly*. doi: 10.1016/j. leaqua.2016.11.007

- engaging in conversations and listening at least twice as much as speaking.

It also suggests a sincere belief that others are more important than one is oneself.

As a junior officer, I watched a more senior officer go out of his way to sit next to the driver of the crew van as we went out to the aircraft. No one else did this. Typically, we all sat together and never talked to the driver except when we thanked them for the ride, but not this extraordinary leader: he chose to spend time with those whom most did not recognize, ensuring that they knew they were appreciated. When you lead from the front and model how vital everyone is to the effort, your agenda is rarely ever challenged.

The reality is that agendas themselves can rarely be explained: actions and behaviors must model them. If followers question a leader's behavior, then the leader has already lost this opportunity. When followers see what drives a leader, they do not question their motives because they understand them. The extraordinary leader I have just referenced was simply the most incredible listener I have ever met. We would engage in conversation and he would always pause for what seemed like an eternity to ensure that I had finished speaking. He cared about everything I had to say.

When a leader makes themself approachable and listens carefully to ensure that their followers are properly heard, agendas are rarely questioned. The leader discussed above eventually rose to the top of his field and, throughout his career, never wavered in his desire for transparent communications. His example became the model for those in his sphere of influence. Having the courage to embrace a level of vulnerability, emotional risk, and exposure reaps the results of developing widespread trust that you can count on. Leaders who make themselves approachable positively influence their immediate followers as well as future leaders and followers for generations to come. It is the law of sowing and reaping—you almost always reap much more than you sow.

The leadership response to the COVID-19 pandemic demonstrated the impact of politically driven motivations, not courageous leadership. It also showed the impact of hidden agendas among various political leaders at both the federal and state levels. Trust between these politicians and within certain jurisdictions was questioned, and differing levels of chaos ensued. The virus's seriousness was never questioned, but there were real questions about what was motivating the leaders in their response to the pandemic. Agendas do matter and, when they are not transparent, those who must follow the directions within them consistently question the leaders' sincerity and distrust their motives.

Shackleton's leadership was not exempt from those in his crew questioning his motives or even rebelling against his leadership despite his transparency. Understanding this point is critical to every leader and would-be leader. What made Shackleton successful was his immediate and direct response to this tension, which, while remaining consistent with his purpose and agenda, preserved the dignity of those who had challenged him.

Takeaway: The law of sowing and reaping suggests that you almost always reap much more than you sow but it does not guarantee that there won't be storms or bugs that will threaten your crop. However, it does ensure that, if you deal with these problems in line with your original purpose and agenda, you will reap a positive return. Compromise in this area can be catastrophic. Those who follow watch out for consistency with eagle eyes. If they find it, they will follow and respect the leader for the exchange between them—this respect is the final essential ingredient if transparency is to be effective.

Questions to consider:

- Why is compromise considered catastrophic when considering transparent communications?

- Why are hidden agendas within an organization so damaging to trust within leader and follower relationship?

Respect for the Exchange

As social creatures, we are always seeking affirmation and security. We tend to affiliate with others who accept us for who we are, or perhaps who they think we are, and we choose to be around those who make us feel safe. These affirmation and security levels seem to go hand in hand as we evaluate relationships based on previous communications and actions, and the apparent motives of those involved.

Going back to David and Mary's example, we see clearly that David was seeking both affirmation and security. By going around the organization having closed-door conversations with his co-workers, he was trying to figure out whether they accepted him and whether he could trust them. Ironically, his actions backfired on him because his motives were called into question.

Encouraging and achieving transparent communications are linear processes that require clarity, followed by an assessment of how consistently the communications are acted on. We all tend to give the benefit of the doubt to others when entering a relationship and we maintain this benefit until an inconsistency occurs that causes us to either doubt the person's sincerity or suspect a hidden agenda. This is easier in an exchange of equals: one of the challenges of assessing inconsistencies lies in recognizing that different generations have different needs for affirmation and security.

A recent study on leadership and generations at work suggests significant differences in what baby boomers and millennials find desirable in leaders. Baby boomers typically value high integrity, fairness, and empowerment as key leadership traits, whereby millennials value team players and motivators as key leader types.[54] Millennials currently occupy most of our

---

54 Rudolph, C., Rauvola, H., & Zacher, H. (2018). Leadership and generations at work: A critical review. *The Leadership Quarterly*, 29(1), 1–65.

lower and mid-level management positions and, by 2025, they are predicted to make up 75% of the global workforce.[55]

With a focus on team play and motivation, millennials place a higher value on affirmation, confidence building, and knowledge than previous generations.[56] This social media generation documents and comments on nearly every facet of their lives, and individuals migrate toward those with similar feelings. Knowing how a generation thinks is essential for its leaders. When we understand generational thought processes, "leadership and followership functions and roles may be traded or exchanged by the positional leaders and followers in different situations or organizational settings toward mutual respect, empowerment, and effectiveness."[57]

Respect for the exchange is all about respect for differences. If relationships are between members with the same ideas, beliefs, and values, there is nothing to trade or exchange. When differences between members are valued and respected, the opportunity for exchange and trade can enhance the relationship and increase organizational effectiveness—perhaps reflecting the team building and motivation that millennials refer to. But the question is: how do people with differing ideas, beliefs, and values even come to the table to discuss these differences?

55 Overdijk, R., & Bos, D. (2017). The Millennial difference: The effect of adapted job resources and HR practices on turnover intentions of Millennials. *Tilburg University*, 1–141.
56 Overdijk & Bos, 'The Millennial difference'.
57 Malakyan, P. (2013). Followership in leadership studies: A case of leader–follower trade approach. *Journal of Leadership Studies*, 7(4), 6–23. doi:10.1002/jls.21306

The answer to this question lies in our attitude about the value of other human beings. In our previous discussions, we talked about the leadership complaint regarding the difficulty of finding good people. I suggested the irony that, when a leader decided to hire an applicant and the applicant decided to accept the job, the arrangement seemed amicable. Each was hopeful for agreement, and each most likely experienced the biological release of dopamine creating the feeling of happiness when the deal was closed. But then what?

The motivational speaker and successful performance coach, Jim Rohn, suggests that, if you are looking for success, find a successful person, take them to lunch, and listen to everything they have to say. While this may sound a little extreme, Jim Rohn points to how success leaves clues and those seeking them must search for them. How often do leaders search for success in those they hire? How often do those hired seek success in those they follow? Ironically, by adopting an attitude of seeking success in those we engage with, we demonstrate respect by affirming one another. When we believe each individual has extraordinary and unique skills, and we value that belief, we affirm their value.

Remember the story at the beginning of this Part V about the trusting leader who empowered his followers to *always tell him what they were thinking and, if they had to, make him listen?* My friend described him as an exceptional leader because he gave them the respect of valuing their opinions and made them feel as if they were critical team members. When members know that their teammates are counting on them, they are motivated to make a special effort to play their part.

Theodore Roosevelt's famous quote, "People don't care how much you know until they know how much you care," is in line with the millennial needs described earlier—teamwork and motivation. Research suggests that leaders can show how much they care by allowing their employees to contribute and make a difference, knowing that their leaders value and respect them as individuals.[58] The fruits of this caring approach are employee commitment, engagement, creativity, and loyalty.[59]

The average person spends eight hours a day in the work environment. In many cases, we spend more time at work than we do with our families. We could easily argue that our work shapes us more than almost anything else we do. When leaders can create a mutually accountable culture, as described in Part IV of this book, employees enjoy the workplace and bring more creativity to performing their job.[60]

Takeaway: Leaders who encourage transparency in communications—by checking for clarity in their guidance and policies; by ensuring that their agendas are transparent and in line with their purpose; and by taking the time to understand their employees' ideas, beliefs, and

58 Miller, L. (2018). *Leader-Employee Relationship as an Antecedent to Employee Commitment Mediating Innovative Work Behavior*. A dissertation presented in partial fulfillment of the requirements for the degree Doctorate of Business Administration, Capella University, Atlanta, Georgia.

59 Miller, *Leader-Employee Relationship*.

60 Phillips, *Perception of Mutual Accountability*.

values—earn the respect of their employees and benefit from the fruits of employee commitment, engagement, creativity, and loyalty. Trust is a by-product of respect, and respect is the reward for leaders who communicate transparently.

The story of the *Endurance* highlights the importance of encouraging transparent communications and, also, why trust matters. Shackleton knew that he could not succeed in this third Antarctic exploration without a crew fully committed to the task and aware of all the dangers and challenges that lay ahead. The crew knew that they needed a leader with the experience and leadership skills that they could trust with their lives. From the first advertisement for a crew that Shackleton sent out, to the last crew member safely returning home, he—and they—knew that he alone was responsible for the lives of those he had been entrusted to lead.

Within the context of a mutually accountable relationship, trust matters because lives depend on it. Leaders have an impact on the livelihood of those they employ and are accountable for that impact. When they take the time to engage their employees transparently, they learn more about the skills and talents they have at hand and can employ them more effectively. At the same time, the employees realize that their leader is interested in them and their development within the team, which motivates them to succeed. This mutual engagement builds trust within the relationship that has a positive impact on the lives of both the leaders and followers.

When leaders realize the accountability they have for those under their influence and the importance of transparent communications, they can take the next step in finding joy in leadership: *establishing relational expectations.* If trust is a by-product of respect, then understanding how trust has an impact on the organization becomes the next step on the journey.

Questions to consider:

- Why don't leaders take the time to fully understand the skills and talents of the people they employ?

- If trust at work matters because lives depend on it, why don't leaders ensure transparent communications in the workplace?

Establishing Relational Expectations: *How* **Trust has an Impact on an Organization**

The senior airline Captain enters the cockpit greeting the First Officer who is already preparing the aircraft by inserting the flight plan, weather, and weight and balance data into the flight management system. The Captain gets settled into his workplace and reviews the flight logbook and paperwork before completing his pre-flight duties. Once both have fulfilled their respective responsibilities, the Captain provides the departure briefing, highlighting the planned course of action for both normal and abnormal situations during the departure.

Before addressing the brief's abnormal situations, the Captain looks directly at the First Officer and says, "I am very easy to fly with, but there is one thing that could really upset me." The First Officer's eyes open wide and his attention is laser-focused on the Captain who continues, "If you see me doing something wrong, or not in accordance with our standard operating procedures, and you don't say something, you will have really let me down."

Establishing relational expectations within a mutually accountable relationship involves developing trust by acknowledging a) that lives depend on it, and b) *how* it has an impact on the organization. Articulating expectations within the relationship takes transparent communications to the next level. When you speak frankly, *saying what you mean and meaning what you say*, the time is ripe to talk about expectations. Unfortunately, in most leader–follower relationships, the *expectation* conversation is typically only one way—from the leader to the follower.

Because a relationship, by nature, is an interactive exchange between two parties, effective relationships are rarely one way.[61] Like transparent communications,

61 Phillips, *Perception of Mutual Accountability.*

establishing relational expectations requires both parties to be honest about who they are and how they feel, even though this makes them vulnerable to expectations from the other side. When the Captain told the First Officer that he expected him to point out his mistakes, he was making himself vulnerable and, at the same time, suggesting the same for the First Officer.

A pivotal point to establishing relational expectations is the importance of conceptualizing relationships as inherently two-way, considering both parties' influence from a mutual perspective.[62] Considering the relationship as two-way doesn't diminish the unique role each plays. Leaders still bear the responsibility of leadership and followers still assume the responsibility of followership. This is why establishing expectations within a relationship is so important. When leaders don't solicit these from their followers, the followers are left wondering whether it is appropriate for them to mention a concern.

We have already established why trust matters because lives are at stake and efforts toward establishing relational expectations take trust building to the next level. The story of Asiana Flight 214 on July 6, 2013, illustrates this point. This trans-Pacific passenger flight from Incheon, South Korea, to San Francisco, California, was in the final landing phase of its flight when the lack of establishing relational expectations created a situation endangering the 307 people on board, eventually injuring 187, and leading to the death of 3.

62 Phillips, *Perception of Mutual Accountability*.

When we don't establish relational expectations, assumptions and initiative are all we have to evaluate actions and motives within a relationship. Also, research suggests that trust within a relationship is "based on expectations that the intentions, words, or actions of their supervisor can be relied on."[63] The critical question is how do we rely on the intentions, words, or actions of another if we are unclear as to their expectations?

The Captain of Asiana Flight 214 was a veteran pilot but new to the Boeing 777. His First Officer was a Check Airman who had years of experience in the 777 and instructed the Captain on this flight. (The role of the Check Airman is to instruct or assess the Captain on the 777 and eventually approve him for operations in the unfamiliar aircraft.) Another experienced pilot was in the jump seat as a Safety Observer also responsible for pointing out any irregularities or concerns. The aircraft was cleared for a visual approach and landing on runway 28L at San Francisco. The Captain accepted the visual approach and aligned the plane for landing.

With tens of thousands of flight hours between the three pilots, we could easily assume that making a visual approach in just about perfect conditions would just be another "walk in the park" for this crew. Unfortunately, assumptions often create false expectations and can lead to dangerous outcomes. The culture within the relationship can make those assumptions even more problematic. On

---

63 Cheng, C., Jiang, D., Cheng B., Riley, J., & Jen, C. (2015). When do subordinates commit to their supervisors? Different effects of perceived supervisor integrity and support on Chinese and American employees. *The Leadership Quarterly*, 26(1), 81–97.

this flight, the Asiana Captain assumed that the Check Airman had the final say and would advise the Captain of any concerns. The Check Airman respected the Captain as his senior within the company and Asian culture, and did not want to dishonor him, so there was also a cultural influence within the flight crew. To add to this, the entire crew was fatigued from the long trans-Pacific flight and was looking for some much-needed rest.

Because relational expectations were unclear and the cockpit's culture typically gave ultimate authority to the Captain, the visual approach and landing became far more than a walk in the park. When the Captain aligned the aircraft with the landing runway and began to configure the aircraft for landing, he ended up too high on the approach profile. To adjust to this profile, he turned off the autopilot and reduced the throttles to initiate a manual landing. (Normally, full automation is used until the aircraft is a mile or so from landing).

The changes made by the Captain demonstrated his overall experience, but his unfamiliarity with the 777 created expectations of the aircraft's automated systems that would prove to be deadly. The Captain assumed that the 777 auto-throttles would remain engaged just as they would have done in his last aircraft. Neither the Check Airman nor the Safety Observer alerted the Captain to the potential problem. The plane ended up getting too low and the throttled power never came back up, resulting in the tail of the aircraft hitting the seawall at the end of the runway, causing it to break off and the aircraft to crash onto the runway.

We discussed above another Captain's departure briefing, which included a straightforward statement that created a relational expectation with his First Officer: "If you see me doing something wrong, or not in accordance with our standard operating procedures, and you don't say something, you will have really let me down." Establishing relational expectations can be as easy as a one- or two-sentence statement, provided it *sets performance expectations, encourages two-way feedback, and cultivates affirmation through predictability.*

Setting Performance Expectations

Remember the 3×5 index card I put together with my goals and desired expectations? This card was my daily reference directing me toward my personal and professional performance growth. However, it didn't address any expectations that my boss might have of me, or what expectations I might have of my boss.

If leaders dare to take the time to develop a culture of mutual accountability, they must cultivate that culture daily. We have established that mutual accountability is not a one-time event but the result of a continuing process of maintaining an intimate awareness of the relationship's actions, holding each other accountable, and knowing that each will look out for and help the other. So, we must not hold our 3×5 cards close to our chest but instead share our goals for mutual support and understanding.

In a fascinating study on the impact of teachers' leadership styles on students' performance, researchers

145

found that students performed best when teachers played an instructional leader role.[64] When a leader is aware of the goals and expectations of a follower and can play an instructional leader role to help them realize those goals, performance skyrockets. The challenge is how to engage the follower so that they will freely discuss their goals and expectations.

Genuine relationships are based on vulnerability. We saw clearly, with the airline Captain who told the First Officer he expected him to point out any mistakes or deviations, how genuine relationships are based on vulnerability. The Captain demonstrated vulnerability by acknowledging his ability to make mistakes and expecting the First Officer to offer his help and support if needed. This strongly supports the case that, when a leader is willing to accept their vulnerability and initiate a discussion of relational expectations, they inspire the follower to do the same.

Leaders committed to developing trust they can count on need to go beyond organizational expectations based on job descriptions and instead determine the motivations, goals, and personal expectations of those they are privileged to lead: in other words, their followers' 3×5 cards. Not every follower aspires to be a leader, but every follower has aspirations they wish to achieve. The only way for leaders to know what their followers aspire to be, or to achieve, is to be aware of their personal goals and expectations.

64 Raza, S., & Sikandar, A. (2018). Impact of leadership style of teacher on the performance of students: An application of Hersey and Blanchard situational model. *Bulletin of Education and Research*, 40(3), 73–94.

We began by discussing the importance of knowing *why* leaders lead and the importance of *why* organizations exist. Another essential element to effective leadership is understanding *why* your followers are following and where they want you to lead them. Some of the most outstanding leaders I have had the opportunity to work for inspired me to embrace knowing that the most important job I could have was the one I was doing at the time. With that understanding, they instructed me on how my job performance could lead to new and greater opportunities.

Understanding followers' expectations and goals gives leaders unique insight into crafting performance expectations tailored to their followers. This helps them to meet organizational expectations through their job performance, and to address their expectations and goals for developing to a higher level. When followers feel that their work makes a difference, they remain committed to the organization and their leaders.

Research suggests that employees voluntarily leave their jobs because of concerns over career development, work–life balance, manager behavior, compensation, well-being, job characteristics, and work environment.[65] Involved leaders can mitigate every one of these preventable categories by being actively engaged in their employee's goals and expectations by tailoring performance expectations to that engagement.

65 Mahan, T., Nelms, D., Bearden, C., & Pearce, B. (2019). 2019 *Retention report*. Work Institute. https://info.workinstitute.com/hubfs/2019%20Retention%20Report/Work%20Institute%20 2019%20Retention%20Report%20final-1.pdf

Also, when employees feel engaged and of value to an organization, attitudes such as innovation, active learning behavior, knowledge sharing, and adaptability emerge as by-products of this performance expectation.[66]

What is so counter-intuitive about this approach is that, by investing more time in developing performance expectations within the leader–follower relationship, one spends less time managing one's employees. When both the leader and follower share the same performance expectations, psychological safety, perceptions of support, and norms of open dialog, they have in place the constructs to guide their relationship and foster the culture of mutual accountability in which trust can flourish.[67]

Michael was a determined and ambitious worker with meticulous attention to detail who genuinely cared about people. His supervisor, Susan, recognized his drive and viewed him as one of her top employees. Susan was an excellent instructional leader and knew that Michael's goal was to have his own company someday, but he still had a lot to learn before he was ready to make that move. Like a great coach, she recognized both strengths and areas for improvement in Michael and looked for development opportunities.

---

66 Motyka, B. (2018). Employee engagement and performance: A systematic literature review. *Academy of Management Review*, 54(3), 227–244.
67 Destler, K. N. (2016). Creating a performance culture. *The American Review of Public Administration*, 46(2), 201–225. doi:10.1177/0275074014545381

Takeaway: When considering performance expectations within a mutually accountable relationship, instructional leaders continually seek development opportunities for their ambitious followers. These opportunities may come in the form of unsolved problems from higher levels of the organization or challenges that lie within the immediate organization. The beauty of human interactions lies in the unique challenges that occur within each relationship. When leaders take the time to discover those opportunities and invest in their followers' expectations, a synergy of ideas emerges from the relationship.

The performance expectation by-products of innovation, active learning, knowledge sharing, and adaptability suggest an open dialog for improvement, and cost savings (or perhaps efficiencies) to be gained in the operation. The *why* of the organization will never die if its employees are always looking for new and innovative ways to keep that *reason for existence* alive and well. The one constant every organization can count on is change, and how it adapts to it often defines success or failure.

The COVID-19 pandemic hit the hospitality sector extremely hard, with many small and large businesses closing their doors, unable to survive the required changes. One large company that continued to thrive during this extreme time of change was Chick-fil-A. Before the pandemic, if you went to a restaurant at lunchtime, the inside ordering and drive-thru would routinely be packed. Despite the crowd, the wait never seemed long and the staff always served you with a smile and heartfelt thanks.

The Chick-fil-A website defines their *why* simply: "We should be about more than just selling chicken. We should be a part of our customers' lives and the communities in which we serve." The chicken is fantastic, but the service is even better. When the pandemic closed off in-store capacity, Chick-fil-A took being a part of their customers' lives to a new level by designing a customer-focused and efficient drive-thru process adhering to all COVID-19 requirements while still serving a large lunchtime crowd.

You need to question the metrics for a 2019 study rating Chick-fil-A as the slowest drive-thru in the industry, because this did not present the full picture.[68] The restaurant was rated the slowest—yes, but only because it had more volume than any other drive-thru in the industry. While the speed may have decreased because of increased volume, the performance did not waver. The same survey also rated Chick-fil-A as best in both accuracy and customer service. The restaurant's ability to adjust to the larger volumes set the stage for their continued excellent support during the pandemic. Its *why* remained the focus despite having to adapt to change.

Within a mutually accountable culture where every member knows *why* they are there and intimately

68 Oches, S. (2019, October 16). The truth about Chick-fil-A's Drive Thru. *QRS Magazine*. https://www.qsrmagazine.com/exclusives/truth-about-chick-fil-drive-thru

understands *how* their actions have an impact on performance expectations, the foundation is laid for the next element of establishing relational expectations— *encouraging two-way feedback*. Once performance expectations are set, both leader and follower have a baseline from which to provide feedback to develop relational expectations further, and to realize *how* trust has an impact on an organization.

Questions to consider:

- When a leader does not set performance expectations, what is the measure by which the follower's performance is evaluated?

- How do the performance expectation by-products of innovation, active learning, knowledge sharing, and adaptability suggest an open dialog for improvement areas?

Encouraging Two-Way Feedback

The Captain parked the aircraft at the gate and shut down the engines, and the crew completed the parking checklist. Once complete, the Captain looked over at the First Officer and said, "So what do you have for me?" The First Officer seemed a little shocked by the question. Typically, in the airline industry, the only time the cockpit door remains closed and the Captain asks for feedback is when something out of the ordinary occurred or didn't go so well.

Feedback can be a powerful tool for achieving our personal and professional goals and realizing expectations. Unfortunately, it is typically only given when something out of the ordinary has occurred or didn't go so well. In these circumstances, it is associated with negativity so that avoiding it instead of seeking it becomes the goal. Also, feedback is typically one way—from a leader to a follower.

The main problem with one-way feedback is that it leads to one of the greatest leadership dangers—power. When leaders are protected against the sanctions that may arise when they violate a social norm, they are more likely to resort to stereotyping and discrimination in their relationships with followers.[69] Within power-focused leadership, followers fear bringing any concerns to the leader's attention and choose to remain silent even if "the emperor has no clothes"!

One-way feedback is not an option for leaders committed to developing a culture of mutual accountability and thereby finding joy in leadership. They must initiate the process by soliciting feedback from their followers, thereby opening the door to constructive *two-way* feedback. Because feedback is inherently perceived

69 Dwertmann, D., & Boehm, S. (2016). Status matters: The asymmetric effects supervisor-subordinate disability incongruence and climate for inclusion. *Academy of Management Journal*, 59(1), 44–64.

as negative, they must be ready to model the process for their followers.

The First Officer looked at the Captain and said, "I thought things went pretty smoothly. I really don't have anything for you." The Captain thanked the First Officer and said, "Well, there were a couple of things that I saw. First, I was a little fast on the arrival, so it made me a little late configuring. It worked out ok, but I ended up carrying about five extra knots crossing the threshold and landed a little beyond the 1,000-foot marker."

By positively demonstrating the necessary level of detail, leaders can model for their followers the feedback process and the desire for continuous self-improvement. The next time a follower is asked for feedback, they will realize that it is not a negative process but a growing and learning opportunity that will help them to reach their goals. Constructive feedback can also lead to an instructional dialog that can benefit both parties, further enhancing trust and encouraging even deeper scrutiny towards improvement.

A great friend and retired Air Force leader described the feedback process within a mutually accountable relationship as the "wingman concept":

The wingman concept means that if you and I are a two-ship, then I'm responsible for your back. You're responsible for mine. One of us is a leader. One of us is in support. We recognize those roles. We're both responsible for mission success. I'm responsible for telling you as a lead that things are not going right. You're responsible for telling me as a wingman that I'm not fulfilling my responsibility. There is no room for candy coating. You've got to be able to provide that feedback and not have it affect the interpersonal relationship and get the mission done.[70]

The key phrase here is *get the mission done*. This is the *why* of leadership and followership that should align with the *why* of the organization. When both parties realize the benefits of two-way feedback, trust is enhanced within the relationship, and each member feels the freedom to give their best knowing that the other has their best interests in mind and will give help and support as needed.

Within a mutually accountable relationship, there also needs to be a justice and grace balance: the concept of accountability suggests a fair and just process. When expectations are established within the relationship, we must assume that those expectations will be realized and, if they are not, that there will be a fair accounting of the circumstances. However, within this accounting, we must also be willing to exercise grace to encourage the best within the future relationship.

---

70 Phillips, *Perception of Mutual Accountability.*

Two-way feedback is the vehicle that delivers this justice and grace balance. Within the leader–follower relationship, honest and constructive feedback can provide a unique insight into areas that might otherwise be blind spots to performance or behavior. Research suggests that feedback among peers provides a valid and reliable source of performance data.[71] While we could argue that there are no peers within a leader–follower relationship, we could also suggest that a unique peer relationship exists in a mutually accountable relationship.

The wingman concept demonstrates the performance reliability suggested by the research.[72] There are still clear leader and follower roles, but there is also an explicit expectation of candid and honest feedback to ensure mission success. When both parties commit to fulfilling their respective roles towards this, mutual accountability supports a peer relationship. During my Air Force career, I received candid and honest feedback on multiple occasions from several of my followers, and I respected and trusted them even more for making me a better leader as a result.

In Part I of this book, we talked about the biological release of dopamine and serotonin. To recap, when we experience happiness, our bodies release dopamine. It is the feeling associated with receiving a gift, buying a new car, or receiving a promotion. These

71 Naseer, S., Raja, U., Syed, F., Donia, M. B. L., & Darr, W. (2016). Perils of being close to a bad leader in a bad environment: Exploring the combined effects of despotic leadership, leader member exchange, and perceived organizational politics on behaviors. *The Leadership Quarterly*, 27(1), 14–33. doi: 10.1016/j.leaqua.2015.09.005

72 Phillips, *Perception of Mutual Accountability*.

are all good feelings but, unfortunately, they quickly fade. In contrast, being accepted and valued within an organization or by your boss creates a longer-term and deeper-rooted sense of approval.

Takeaway: When we feel approval, our bodies release both dopamine and serotonin. The feeling lasts much longer and we start to identify ourselves with those who accept and value us. Candid and constructive two-way feedback enhances organizational trust while encouraging continuous self-reflection and self-improvement. It's easy to remember a favorite teacher or mentor who provided feedback and encouraged us to be the best we could be. When others take the time to constructively help us to improve, we form a bond with them. That bond is associated with the biological release of serotonin.

Shackleton developed a strong bond with his crew members by his force of character. His transparent communications, commitment to treating each member fairly, and holding each of them accountable created a bond of acceptance that endured even the harshest of conditions. The true measure of leadership effectiveness is often portrayed in adversity. When an organization is in a very difficult or dangerous situation, how does it perform? It would be hard to imagine a situation worse than the one Shackleton faced when it became clear that the expedition was not going to make it to the South Pole and the challenge became all about survival.

When leaders realize the value of two-way feedback and model it for their followers, they enhance relational expectations and build a deeper trust within the relationship. Like a checkbook balance, trust determines the extent that leaders can draw on the organization in times of peril and uncertainty. By investing in their followers through performance expectations and two-way feedback, leaders demonstrate the impact that trust has within an organization. The last key point in establishing relational expectations and showing *how* trust has such an impact is *cultivating affirmation through predictability*, as discussed below.

Questions to consider:

- How does constructive two-way feedback enhance trust within a relationship, and how does that have an impact on an organization?

- Why is a justice and grace balance important within a mutually accountable relationship where two-way feedback is provided?

Cultivating Affirmation Through Predictability

Part III addressed the human needs for affirmation, security, and trust in relationships. The takeaway was the importance for leaders to understand the balance between humans' need for affirmation and security and their innate desires to control their domain. In Part IV, we discussed the importance of developing a culture of mutual accountability where transparency, predictability, and growth flourish. Within the culture of mutual accountability, and specifically in establishing relational expectations, leaders can cultivate affirmation throughout the organization by the predictability of their actions.

From an infant's cry to be fed to our adult desire to realize our purpose on this earth, human beings seek to control their domain and realize harmony with their circumstances. This harmony has been described as finding our niche, discovering our dream, or living our purpose. It is that feeling of belonging, being comfortable within one's skin, or, in other words, completely free to be "you". For the artist, it is their authentic presentation; for the scientist, it is discovering new truths and theories; and for an athlete, it is the superior performance of their skills. Harmony is the expression of affirmation developed through discipline, hard work, passion, and a thirst for feedback.

We can only view the harmony within our lives when we can count on our body and mind to perform at their trained levels. It is the *calmness* that commentators use to ascribe to athletes when they perform at the highest levels; or the *ease* with which an artist strokes their brush or a violinist plays their instrument as viewers watch in awe of their talent and effortless performance.

This harmony or affirmation comes from the predictability developed from tireless hours of practice and repetition in our quest to be the best we can be. Thus, a key question to be considered is where does this quest come from? Certainly, after some time, it would seem to come from a passion inside one, but what sparked this fire in the first place? The answer is a leader or mentor who took the time to see a unique quality in someone and then cultivated that quality over time. In simple terms, before someone can believe in themselves, someone else has to believe in them.

During my initial jet training, I was paired with an instructor who was frustrated that he had not been selected to be a fighter pilot and instead was *burdened* with teaching the primary jet fundamentals to new students. His frustration was evident to all his students because, no matter how well they performed a maneuver, he made sure that they knew they would never be as good as he was—that is, if he let them make it that far. As one of his students, every day was about surviving for another day. We were never affirmed as pilots, let alone as aspiring individuals.

To my good fortune, halfway through the primary jet program, I was scheduled with a guest pilot to perform on an instrument simulator. This pilot had come back to the training environment after two operational tours and had clocked up thousands of hours, including some in combat. As we went through the lesson requirements, this combat-seasoned instructor said something that changed my aviation life. He said: "By the end of this program, you will be able to fly these instruments better than I can!" I couldn't believe it: he had affirmed me as a pilot and believed that I could be better than he was. He made me feel as though he saw something in me that was greater than I saw in myself!

What makes this story so noteworthy is the affirmation in just one meeting with a true leader because it was clear that he believed in my abilities. The non-affirming predictability of the past was replaced with affirmation and hope for the future. This consistency by the leader in setting performance expectations and encouraging two-way feedback demonstrates investment and belief in the follower. These then cultivate acceptance and affirmation, encouraging trust and positively influencing relational expectations.

Remember Mark from our personal and professional growth discussion in Part II? As a millennial, affirmation and leaders who motivated were both essential to Mark. His suggestion of moving to a four-day workweek and volunteering to fill the open manager's position reflected his need to make a difference within the organization and to contribute to its success. His supervisor, Sally, recognizing the importance of setting performance expectations and providing two-way feedback, suggested that Mark should vet the idea of a four-day workweek with his peers and report back to her with the results. She also recognized Mark's initiative and realized that this was an opportunity to develop that initiative and explore his leadership potential.

Because Sally took the time to consider these two possibilities and discuss them with Mark, Mark realized that there were more things to consider (performance expectations) before she could decide (by initiating two-way feedback). Mark was affirmed in his position and encouraged by both suggestions. Sally demonstrated support for Mark's initiatives and the predictability of her response would encourage him to strive harder in the future.

Great leaders demand excellence from themselves and their followers, and they welcome feedback to allow their teams to realize their greatest potential. Cultivating affirmation is a two-way street when it comes to relational expectations. Leadership is as much an art as a science. Therefore, leaders must pay attention to the outcomes of their approaches, and then assess and refine them as needed to cultivate both their own leadership performance and their followers' potential.

Takeaway: Cultivating affirmation is a continuous cycle of articulating performance expectations, providing two-way constructive feedback, and assessing the results. Just as a sports team sets goals for the season, reviews the videos from each week's performance, and then considers the way ahead, so do those in mutually accountable relationships in which relational expectations are established. The predictability of this continuous self-improvement cycle enables those concerned to learn more and more about themselves and to recognize their expanded potential and newfound trust. In Part VI, we will look at the final two by-products of Developing Trust You Can Count On: *What* trust does for the relationship and *Who* we become in that relationship.

Questions to consider:

- How has trust, or a lack of trust, between you and your supervisor had an impact on your performance within the organization?

- Why is predictability important within the leader–follower relationship?

Part V Recap:
Developing Trust You Can Count On
The Why and The How

Encouraging Transparent Communications: Why Trust Matters

- *Clarity for decision-making* requires that the leader knows why they lead and who they are accountable to for that leadership. They listen for clarity in their guidance and policies to assess transparency.
- Transparent communication from a *purpose versus agenda* perspective demands that leaders make themselves visible and listen carefully to ensure that their followers are heard, and that their leadership agendas are transparent and in line with their purpose.
- *Respect for the exchange* is the by-product of leaders taking the time to understand their employees' ideas, beliefs, and values, earning their respect, and gaining the fruits of employee commitment, engagement, creativity, and loyalty.

Establishing Relational Expectations: How Trust has an Impact on an Organization

- When considering *performance expectations* within a mutually accountable relationship, instructional leaders continually seek development opportunities for their ambitious followers. When leaders take the time to discover those opportunities and invest in their followers' expectations, a synergy of ideas emerges from the relationship.
- When leaders realize the value of *two-way feedback* and model that to their followers, they enhance relational expectations and build deeper trust within their relationships.
- *Cultivating affirmation* is a continuous cycle of articulating performance expectations, providing two-way constructive feedback, and assessing the results.

Part VI:

Developing Trust You Can Count On

The What and The Who

We discovered that, when leaders check for clarity in their guidance and policies, ensure that their agendas are transparent and in line with their purpose, and take the time to understand their employees' ideas, beliefs, and values, they earn the respect of their employees and demonstrate *why* trust matters in every relationship. Also, when leaders set performance expectations, ensure constructive two-way feedback, and cultivate affirmation by continually engaging their employees in a predictable manner, they demonstrate the way in which that trust has an impact (the *how)* on the organization. Now it is time to look at the by-product of that trust: *enhancing personal and professional growth*: *what* trust does for a relationship.

Enhancing Personal and Professional Growth: *What* Trust Does for a Relationship

In Part IV, we challenged you to dare to be different by taking the time to develop a culture of mutual accountability. By developing an intimate awareness of the effects of their actions on another, and holding each other accountable for progress and outcomes, leaders can cultivate the fruits of enhanced trust within their organization. It is this trust within the workforce that can move an organization from good to great, ordinary to extraordinary, and surviving to thriving.

The proposal manager for the Service Disabled Small Business team entered the conference room and presented the options for new work orders open for bidding in the coming weeks. One of the work orders stood out from the rest. It was a high-value opportunity in the Washington DC area where a large aerospace technology company had performed for over a decade. Initially, the team, consisting of representatives from a dozen like-minded integrity-focused companies, suggested that pursuing the work of a billion-dollar aerospace technology company might be too ambitious.

As we have just finished discussing, trust within mutually accountable relationships unleashes untapped potential to accomplish what would previously have been thought to be too ambitious—if not impossible. The United States of America was the first country to land a man on the moon because President John F. Kennedy created the vision, laid down a timeline, believed in the NASA professionals, and consistently kept his promise to support and advocate for them. Research suggests that, when leaders provide a learning culture and growth mindset, a multitude of benefits surface to include accelerating the successful implementation of strategic objectives.[73]

The race to the moon is one illustration of the impact trust from a mutually accountable relationship—based on such a culture and mindset—can have on an organization. The record-setting development of a vaccine for COVID-19 also points to President Trump creating a vision, laying down a timeline, believing in the pharmaceutical professionals, and consistently backing up his promise with support and advocacy. Due to this vision, the country developed not one but three approved vaccines in under a year!

Research shows that growth mindsets support development initiatives by setting specific goals and targets to realize expectations above and beyond typical work issues.[74] In other words, teams can achieve well beyond their currently constrained expectations by the way they think and their state of mind. The mindset of considering how to do so is captured in Napoleon Hill's book *Think and Grow Rich*[75], where he quotes a portion of Walter D. Wintle's famous "It's All In The State of Mind":

---

73 Susing, I. (2016). Coaching at the top optimizing the impact of senior leaders. *OD Practitioner*, 48(4), 13–19.
74 Susing, 'Coaching at the top'.
75 Hill, N. (1972). *The think and grow rich action pack*. Hawthorn Books.

If you think you are beaten, you are.
If you think you dare not, you don't.
If you like to win, but you think you can't,
It is almost certain you won't.

If you think you'll lose, you're lost.
For out in the world we find,
Success begins with a fellow's will—
It's all in the state of mind.

If you think you are outclassed, you are,
You've got to think high to rise,
You've got to be sure of yourself before
You can ever win a prize.

Life's battles don't always go
To the stronger or faster man.
But soon or late, the man who wins
Is the man WHO THINKS HE CAN!

The proposal manager for the Service Disabled Small Business team acknowledged the challenges in unseating a solid incumbent with vastly more resources than existed within this team and then posed the question, "If we were to unseat this incumbent, how would we do it?" The team members looked around the room with smiles on their faces because they knew they would go after this opportunity. Their proposal's success began with that look and ended a few weeks later when the team was awarded the work. The team went on to support the Washington, DC National Capital Region in exemplary fashion for years, all because they had a vision, believed they could realize it, and kept every promise they had made in the proposal.

The path to achieving success is paved by leaders who provide the vision and inspiration to influence followers to extend their goals and perform beyond the expectations specified in their formal work roles and job descriptions.[76] It is founded on accepting that there is always room for improvement, seeking new ways, and trying out ideas for achieving what seems unachievable. This path less traveled discourages the faint of heart because it requires us to leave the comforts of what is known and move from the accepted into the unknown and not yet experienced.

Neil Armstrong's famous quote: "That's one small step for man, one giant leap for mankind," illustrates the benefits of exploring the unknown and achieving beyond our perceived constraints. In addition to the remarkable feat of landing a man on the moon, the collateral benefits continue serving us to this day. Modern commercial aircraft, including the Airbus 320 series and Boeing

---

76 Qu, R., Janssen, O., & Shi, K. (2017). Leader–member exchange and follower creativity: The moderating roles of leader and follower expectations for creativity. *International Journal of Human Resource Management*, 28(4), 603–626.

737 upgrades, employ digital fly-by-wire technology developed during the Apollo years. NASA also developed the food-packaging techniques used today to ensure our food safety. The *moon blankets* that every marathon finisher is wrapped in at the end of a race are products of our quest to explore. Thus, the vision to take a small step truly can provide a giant leap for humankind.

At every level of achievement, a certain degree of trust must be relied upon. From the food we eat, to the cars we drive, to the air we breathe, we trust we can go safely about our lives and realize our dreams. The COVID-19 pandemic has shaken this trust because of the inconsistencies of transparent communications from our leaders and scientists, as well as the lack of affirming how we are to go about leading our lives safely in this new era of unknowns. Perhaps now more than ever, we need leaders to demonstrate actions that reflect the trust we need to overcome these unknowns. By inspiring creativity and ingenuity, developing character, and realizing potential in their followers, leaders enhance trust within their organization and demonstrate *what* trust does for humanity.

Inspire Creativity and Ingenuity

We only need to think about the evolution of the personal computer or the proliferation of smartphones to realize the impact and influence of creativity and ingenuity. In January 2007, Steve Jobs introduced the iPhone, suggesting it was years ahead of its time. Today, according to a study done by

Oberlo.com, 4 out of every 10 human beings on the planet own a smartphone.[77] Thus, in nearly 14 years, the vision inspired by a man who wanted to put a personal computer in the hands of every human being has been realized and has revolutionized our day-to-day lives.

Steve Jobs did not do all of this on his own. He had a vision that inspired creativity and ingenuity in those within his sphere of influence, and now that sphere of influence has grown to over 130,000 full-time employees. If you have ever been to an Apple store, you have experienced the enthusiasm and loyalty each employee working there has for this company. Apple employees are not just trained to do their jobs: they are inspired to use their creativity and ingenuity to understand their customers' problems and provide effective solutions.

Today's post-COVID-19 world looks very different from the one we lived in before this virus invaded our borders. While mask-wearing and maintaining social distances have become optional, a climate of fear still lingers amid a growing skepticism regarding the restrictions of the past. Perhaps now, more than ever, leaders need to inspire creativity and ingenuity in every facet of our new realities. George Kneller's famous quote on creativity could not be more appropriate than at a time such as this:

Creativity, as has been said, consists largely of rearranging what we know in order to find out

---

77 5 Oberlo.com (2020). How many people have smartphones in 2021? https://www.oberlo.com/statistics/how-many-people-have-smartphones

what we do not know. Hence, to think creatively, we must be able to look afresh at what we normally take for granted.[78]

Research suggests that creativity and innovation are catalysts for progress and give organizations a competitive edge.[79] But progress and competitive edge must be redefined and re-examined in the post-COVID-19 workplace. Leaders must critically evaluate their organizations and, perhaps more importantly, the reason they were formed in the first place. All of this goes back to our conversation about *why* leaders lead and *why* organizations exist—as discussed in Parts I and IV.

Similar to the abrupt stop to our lives and routines due to the global pandemic and the closing of the economy, Shackleton and his crew's lives came to an abrupt stop when the ice closed in on the *Endurance*. The ice eventually crushed the ship that had been their home and shelter for months. Now they were forced to abandon the expedition to the South Pole, shift to survival mode, and creatively develop a plan to get everyone back to England. Some might say it was a miracle that everyone survived the *Endurance* experience. I would say that it was Shackleton's leadership and his ability to inspire the will, creativity, and ingenuity of his crew.

Leaders who are in touch with *why* they lead realize that they depend on solutions within the

---

78 George Kneller quotes—Art-quotes. http://www.art-quotes.com/auth_search. php?authid=5769#.YOMhf9tMGmk

79 Hughes, D., Lee, A., Wei Tan, A., Newman, A., & Legood, A. (2018). Leadership, creativity, and innovation: A critical review and practical recommendations. The Leadership Quarterly, 29(5), 1–88.

organization coming from the creativity and ingenuity of those they lead. In fact, successful leadership depends less on the leader's ability to solve the problems that arise within the organization, and more on their character and the relationships they develop with their followers. Tony Robbins, well-known entrepreneur, best-selling author, and so-called "CEO Whisperer," suggests that leadership is 80% psychology and 20% skills.[80]

The 80% psychology comes from leaders knowing their people and their skill sets, and inspiring them to rearrange "what we know in order to find out what we do not know" (George Kneller).[81] When it became apparent that Shackleton's crew would have to abandon ship and make their way across the ice to safety, Shackleton brought them together, explained the situation, and instructed them to make an inventory of the resources they could take from the ship. They then creatively came up with a plan to reach Elephant Island in the South Shetland Islands.[82]

It would take over five months from conceiving this plan to reach Elephant Island, which they did by drifting on ice floes and eventually using the rescue boats from the ship.[83] Thus, the *Endurance* story highlights that inspiring creativity and ingenuity is critical to improvising and rearranging what is known in order to address what is

---

80 Mann, S. (2017, September 28). Tony Robbins says success is only 20% skill—and the rest is all in your head. *INC.* https://www.inc.com/sonya-mann/tony-robbins-says-entrepreneurship-is-not-for-everyone.html

81 George Kneller quotes.

82 Ward, P., Sir Ernest Shackleton Endurance Expedition Trans-Antarctica 1914–1917. https://www.coolantarctica.com/Antarctica%20fact%20file/History/Shackleton-Endurance-Trans-Antarctic_expedition.php

83 Ward, 'Sir Ernest Shackleton'.

unknown. This is often referred to as "making something out of nothing". When leaders have established trust with their followers, they can draw solutions from within the group by creating a climate that promotes creativity and ingenuity.

Takeaway: In a 2016 study on the effects of ethical leadership and climates for innovation and creativity, researchers found that, when leaders are perceived as ethical, this improves creativity in the work environment, encouraging followers to offer suggestions and opinions, ultimately inspiring novel ideas that unexpectedly become innovative solutions.[84] When trust exists within a relationship, followers feel the security and affirmation they need to think unconventionally and to suggest creative and ingenious solutions. Thus, the leader's role is to create that environment of trust and security that will inspire their followers to develop such solutions.

When the Serviced Disabled Small Business team decided to go after the National Capital Region's work and compete against the billion-dollar large aerospace company, they brought the entire team into the conference room to brainstorm how to approach this opportunity. Fortunately, this team had been together for well over a year, and had already experienced both success and failure when competing for other projects.

84 Chen, A., & Hou, Y. (2016). The effects of ethical leadership, voice behavior and climates for innovation on creativity: A moderated mediation examination. *The Leadership Quarterly,* 27(1), 1–13. doi:10.1016/jleaqua2015.10.007

The team's premise was integrity, and there was a strong sense of trust both within the team generally and between team members. As the team was put together, each member committed to the ideals of service before self and to providing responsive, cost-effective solutions. The entire team believed in this approach and was committed to it. So, when they all brainstormed strategies to win the work, they focused on what responsive, cost-effective solutions would resonate with this customer. The proposed solutions included a new approach to communications and accessibility, and a demonstrated expertise in the National Capital Region.

Because of their creative and cost-effective approach, along with a solid understanding of the requirements and the process for meeting them, this Small Business team was awarded the work. A collateral benefit of the trust within the relationship that had inspired creativity and ingenuity was that it ensured a collective and committed effort to succeed by all involved. The team's efforts in the first year resulted in its members being acknowledged by the customer for their exceptional performance.

Enhancing personal and professional growth by inspiring creativity and ingenuity reinforces purpose within an organization—in other words, the *why* the employees come to work each day. As the culture for creativity and ingenuity grows, so do innovative solutions and a competitive edge. In a 2018 study of 187 leader–follower relationships, the findings emphasized that, when a trustworthy leader establishes environments where followers feel free to share ideas and knowledge, creativity flourishes.[85] In addition to inspiring creativity and ingenuity, trust manifested in personal and professional growth develops individual character.

Questions to consider:

- Why is it important for followers to feel free to express their creativity and ingenuity?

- What are the by-products of this freedom of expression to the organization and the individual?

Developing Character

In Part I, we described the difference between reputation and character. We said that reputation is how others view us and character is who we really are. When we think of character, we typically think of virtues like faithfulness, moderation, self-control, respectability, hospitality, and trustworthiness.[86] While there are numerous approaches to understanding and defining character, for this discussion, we will define character as a set of virtues that are universally accepted as being essential to well-being and excellence.[87]

---

85 Park, H., Choi, Y., & Kim, D. (2018). Leader behavioral integrity, coworker knowledge sharing, and employee creativity. *Seoul Journal of industrial Relations*, 25–47.

86 Bible, New International Version, 2016, (1 Timothy 3:1–13).

87 Sturm, R. E., Vera, D., & Crossan, M. (2017). The entanglement of leader character and leader competence and its impact on performance. *The Leadership Quarterly*, 28(3), 349–366. doi: 10.1016/j.leaqua.2016.11.007

If character is who we really are, then perhaps some introspection is warranted. What virtues would you list that are non-negotiable for you? For those who know you best, what virtues would they list? Would the lists be the same? As suggested earlier, harmony in life could be described as reputation and character being congruent. For leaders who wish to experience the joy of leading, demonstrating consistency in character is vital.

Once again, the inconsistency of behavior in the small business owner described in Part I highlighted this point. He changed his focus from one centered on integrity to one concentrating on money by laying off many of the core employees who had helped build the company from the ground up. This single decision lost the trust of both the employees and customers who had bought into the integrity-centered focus that had previously characterized the company.

This scenario is typical of a company that has lost its reputation or is now seen to be untrustworthy. Inconsistencies in character not only have an impact on an individual: they also affect those around them. A 2018 study on ethical leadership and employee success found a direct relationship between consistency in moral character and a motivated and empowered workforce.[88]

When leaders model and promote positive character, they invest not only in those they lead but

---

88 Dust, S. B., Resick, C. J., Margolis, J. A., Mawritz, M. B., & Greenbaum, R. L. (2018). Ethical leadership and employee success: Examining the roles of psychological empowerment and emotional exhaustion. *The Leadership Quarterly*, 29(5), 570–583. doi:10.1016/j. leaqua.2018.02.002

also the organization's longevity. A shared leadership theme in the military was to train your replacement. In other words, leaders were charged with developing those perceived as future leaders, and specifically identifying and training those who could take over from them when they themselves moved on to other positions. Leading by example is a powerful way to teach those around you, so long as the leadership you are modeling is the type of leadership you wish to foster.

In Part IV, the idea of leading by example was typified by a leader and mentor I was fortunate to serve with, and who was also a fantastic listener. Whether it was the janitor cleaning the building, the crew van driver, or the crew chief putting the chocks under the wheels of the aircraft, this leader went out of his way to engage in the lives of those he came across. He made sure that those who felt invisible in the organization knew that they were visible to him, and he affirmed them as individuals. The sincerity of his actions was never questioned because of the consistency of his interest.

This leader taught thousands how to invest in the people around them, whether they were in direct line through their work or just acquaintances. He never had to say a word to any of these people he taught because his actions spoke loudly. He knew that the consistency and sincerity of his character provided the foundation for his leadership influence, and his effectiveness spoke for itself.

The joy of leadership is directly related to the positive influence leaders have on those they have the privilege to lead. Modeling being faithful, moderate, self-controlled, respectable, hospitable, and trustworthy can inspire others to be the same, having an impact not only within the workplace and the leader–follower relationship but also on families, neighborhoods, and communities. How to make the most substantial impact cannot be drawn from a speech or even from the policies and procedures that leaders craft or implement—instead, it is demonstrated in the character leaders model to those under their direct influence.

Leaders of strong character inspire their followers with an appreciation of their work and by expressing their expectations for the organization. A study on the influences of work characteristics and employees' psychological health found that "regardless of a leader's defined sphere of influence and power in relation to objective work characteristics, leaders also influence employees' perceptions of their work."[89]

Perhaps the most significant way leaders influence their followers about the importance of their work is by explaining why that work is essential to the organization. We have discussed throughout this book the importance of *why*—*why* leaders lead, *why* an organization exists, and *why* followers follow. The consistency of virtues demonstrated in *why* we do the things we do is the glue that holds an organization together and gives each member purpose in what they do.

---

89 Karanika-Murray, M., Bartholomew, K., Williams, G., & Cox, T. (2015). Leader-member exchange across two hierarchical levels of leadership: Concurrent influences on work characteristics and employee psychological health. *Work & Stress*, 29(1), 57–74. doi: 10.1080/02678373.2014.1003994

The young airman stood attentively inside her 6×6-foot guard shack in the middle of winter at Minot Air Force Base, North Dakota, guarding a B-52 Stratofortress. The winter temperatures can drop as low as 16 degrees below zero to a high of 40 degrees. Fortunately for our young airmen, there is a space heater inside the guard shack and a door to keep the wind out. The shifts are typically eight hours, with short breaks each hour, and the supervisor comes around a couple of times during each shift to check on the troops.

While the space heater is an essential item for warmth and morale, even more critical are the supervisors' visits when the supervisor has the opportunity to explain how important the job is in ensuring the safety and security of this multi-million-dollar aircraft. It is a national asset—part of the nuclear triad (missiles, submarines, and bombers) that ensures America's deterrence against any outside nuclear threat. Because of the consistent information and modeled leadership during the supervisors' visits, this young airman is proud of the work she does and the pride in her posture says it all.

If true character is tested during adversity, then it grows with resistance. The universal virtues that make up character are continually challenged in the world we live in. Take a politician who runs for election on a platform of promises only to explain later that circumstances have changed and those "promises" no longer apply. Even worse were the frequent leadership hypocrisies in handling COVID-19 responses when governors mandated state lock-down and public gatherings only to be spotted at fancy restaurants in large gatherings doing just the opposite.

This one example illustrates a failure in the three virtues of honesty, trustworthiness, and integrity. Being a person of character defined by universally accepted virtues requires a constant effort to resist the worldly temptations that can jeopardize our virtues and character at the same time. Like lifting weights, if you want to grow in strength, you must overcome the inherent resistance of larger challenges to build character that can resist the negative influences in the world. Dr. Martin Luther King made this point, stating: "The ultimate measure of a man is not where he stands in moments of comfort and convenience, but where he stands at times of challenge and controversy."

Who we really are and the character that defines us is actually an international theme used to identify ethical leadership. In a fascinating study on American, Asian, and European perspectives on ethical leadership, character was a universally dominant ethical leadership theme.[90] In each geographic region, character ranked

90 Resick, C., Martin, G., Keating, M., Dickson, M., Kwan, H., & Peng, C. (2011). What ethical leadership means to me: Asian, American, and European perspectives. *Journal of Business Ethics*, 101(3), 435-457. doi:10.1007/s10551-010-0730-8

higher than accountability, consideration and respect for others, fairness, collective orientation, and openness and flexibility.[91]

The fact that character is at the top of several different cultures' leadership themes is a point not to be taken casually. Today's social media-focused world allows us to bypass another's character and assume that they must be a good person because they think the way we do. I mean, seriously, if their blog has millions of "likes," they must be credible, right? The challenges the social media world brings about center on acceptance much more than character and, if someone's character is challenged, all we have to do is *fact-check* it. The question then becomes, what is the character of the fact-checker?

Takeaway: The point of all this is that leaders may be in the best position to make a positive difference to their communities' character. They have the opportunity to model character and thus persuade those within their spheres of influence to do the same. Today's polarized world all too often judges us by our political affiliation, the color of our skin, or our religious preference. If Dr King were here today, he might suggest that we have strayed as a society and remind us of his hallmark quote: "I look to a day when people will not be judged by the color of their skin, but by the content of their character." The content of their character that Dr King refers to is not who people think they are, what they look like, or the title they hold—it is who they really are: the virtues they reflect or don't reflect.

---

91 Resick, C. et al., 'What ethical leadership means to me'.

We defined character as a set of universally accepted virtues essential to well-being and excellence.[92] Research supports the fact that character is universally important, and especially so for ethical leaders. Perhaps now more than ever, leaders must decide what virtues they reflect to those within their sphere of influence and what virtues are lacking within their organizations. When leaders focus on enhancing personal and professional growth, the trust built within the relationship inspires creativity, develops character, and facilitates the realization of potential, which is perhaps the greatest possible gift from a leader to a follower.

Questions to consider:

- What character traits or virtues are essential for leaders in the workplace?

- How can establishing a culture of mutual accountability enhance character development and personal and professional growth?

Realizing Potential

There is a Cherokee Indian belief that the medicine you need is in your fist, and to receive it you have to open your hand and release it. The realization of any potential, whether that is our own healing or the ability to achieve our ultimate goals, requires a significant amount of trust. When leaders invest in their followers by encouraging transparent communications, establishing relational expectations, and enhancing personal and professional

92 Sturm et al., 'Entanglement of leader character'.

growth, they create a trust that allows those followers to "open their hands" and release that potential.

Like a coach assessing a team's capabilities, leaders need to determine the talents of those they have the privilege to lead, as well as evaluating their abilities and possibilities for the future. Each of us has an internal desire to realize our dreams but, all too often, life gets in the way, and we become sidetracked and unable to navigate our way toward the realization of our potentials. Leaders see their followers for who they are and have the opportunity to visualize who they might become.

Our dreams are often confused by the challenges of day-to-day life. It becomes difficult to untangle our thoughts for the future, let alone consider the possibility of realizing our full potential. Daily needs consume our conscience and our muddled dreams seem to move to the subconscious, waiting to be discovered and untangled. It often takes someone we trust to identify them to clarify our path and future potential.

Before the simulator flight with the guest instructor, I believed in my abilities as a pilot and was focused on successfully completing my training. Unfortunately, because of the poor attitude of my primary instructor, some doubts clouded my mind. Indeed, these doubts took root, challenging my ability to see my potential clearly.

Leaders have the good fortune to see situations at face value, and their judgment is typically not clouded by their followers' self-doubts and anxieties. By seeing potential in this way, they can convey faith in their followers by providing the needed affirmation and encouragement that allows *the hand to open* and the untapped potential to emerge. When my guest instructor suggested that I would fly instruments better than he could by the end of the program, my previous thoughts about the future were untangled and I could see my potential for success.

By believing in a follower's future growth or potential, a leader provides psychological empowerment that allows them to overcome their self-doubt and realize their potential for success. A recent study found that leaders who model ethical practices bring out the best in their employees through the psychological empowerment that facilitates their current success and future potential.[93] As we discussed in Part IV, creating a culture of mutual accountability provides psychological empowerment whereby employees believe that their dreams can come true.

As has been stated several times throughout this book, the COVID-19 pandemic has changed the workplace and the world we live in. Social interactions have been strictly reduced. Even with three vaccines currently available, moving about freely and interacting in large gatherings must still be undertaken with caution to mitigate the perceived risks and potential variants of the virus. Clearly, safety in the workplace has taken on a new facet.

---

93 Dust et al., 'Ethical leadership and employee success'.

Accomplishing organizational tasks with the same vigor and success will require leaders to empower their followers to develop new and innovative ways to complete their tasks within these new constraints, and to grow the business despite these challenges. In a 2019 article in the *Journal of Developing Areas*, the authors from Australia and Vietnam found that, when followers trust their leaders and are empowered by them, safety within the workplace is enhanced.[94]

When Sully made the split-second decision to land the Airbus 320 on the Hudson, the crew trusted their Captain who had empowered them to do their jobs. The same holds true for Shackleton's crew. When he and a handful of others left Easter Island to find help, those left behind trusted in his return and were empowered to ensure the safety and survival of those with whom they were entrusted.

Inside every person lies an untapped potential just waiting to be discovered. Often it takes the encouragement and insight of a trusted leader to bring that potential out. Anthony Robles knows about realizing untapped potential. Born with only one leg, he had a hard time fitting in with those around him. When he decided to go for wrestling as a young man, he finally found a place where he could be himself, knowing that all he had to rely on were his ability and drive.

The drive to achieve is a choice, and sometimes it is challenging to get out of the valley when life continues

94 Muchiri, M., McMurray, A., Nkhoma, M., & Pham, H. (2019). How transformational and empowering leader behaviors enhance workplace safety: A review and research agenda. *Journal of Developing Areas*, 53(1), 257–265.

to suggest that it may be too difficult. This is where great coaches and leaders encourage and motivate those in the valleys to climb out and pursue the summit. Anthony Robles had just such a high school coach who recognized his drive and helped him reach the summit of high school wrestling and recruitment to a Division I school, Arizona State University (ASU).

After a very successful high school wrestling career when he rarely lost, Anthony struggled to win at the Division I college level. His coach sat him down and said he needed to analyze why he was getting defeated, and to figure out how to overcome any liabilities by maximizing his assets. These conversations never took into account that Anthony had only one leg! Instead, they focused on leveraging his strengths and minimizing his weaknesses!

Takeaway: When trust exists between leaders and followers in a mutually accountable relationship, leaders feel free to challenge and push their followers to discover their potential, and followers are willing to take the risk of "opening their hands" to realize that potential. Because of the trust Anthony Robles had in his coach, he realized his full potential as a college wrestler, becoming a Division I champion at ASU and an inspiration for one-, two-, and no-legged wrestlers and athletes across the country! Let there be no doubt that those who had the privilege to coach and lead Anthony experienced the joy in that leadership and were blessed to see the fruits of that privilege.

Developing trust leaders and followers can count on requires an understanding of *why* trust matters, *how* trust has an impact on an organization, and *what* trust does. By encouraging transparent communications through clarity in decision-making, establishing purpose in the relationship, and maintaining respect for the exchange, followers see *why* trust matters. When relational expectations are established through performance expectations on both sides, providing constructive feedback, and cultivating affirmation through predictability, followers can see *how* trust has an impact on the organization. And, by enhancing personal and professional growth by inspiring creativity, developing character, and realizing potential, followers can see *what* trust does. The final step in developing trust leaders and followers can count on is by experiencing ownership that allows followers to see *who* they can become.

Questions to consider:

- Why is trust so important in realizing our potential and overcoming preconceived notions that may hold us back?

- What role does psychological empowerment play in realizing our potential, and how does leader–follower trust influence empowerment?

Experiencing Ownership and Trust: *Who* We Become

The small business CEO entered the conference room and sat at the head of the table. Also seated at the table were each of her division chiefs and directors, a total of seven. She began the meeting by acknowledging the trust and faith she had in everyone in the room. They had been together for over a decade, endured previous challenging times, and enjoyed more than their share of successes. Today's challenge was something they had never experienced before: the dynamics of a global pandemic accentuated by inconsistent government policies and unpredictable market behavior.

When leaders have taken the time to consistently communicate transparently, establish two-way relational expectations, and invest in their followers' personal and professional growth, ownership and trust become the by-products of their labor. We introduced the concept of ownership in our discussion of the inherent challenges associated with leadership in Part II. When we spoke of a private pilot making their first solo flight, ownership was described as that point where the leader trusts that the follower has been appropriately mentored and instructed, has internalized the information, and is ready to implement it on their own.

This internalized ownership, sometimes referred to as "psychological ownership," is defined as a follower's feeling or belief that they have a responsibility to make decisions in the organization's long-term best interest and are accountable for those decisions.[95] Just as taking physical ownership of a car or a home, psychological ownership suggests a state of mind in which we feel as though we have ownership, whether that be of a novel idea, strategic initiative, or a specific project.[96] In simple terms, the buck stops with the follower as the owner: they accept responsibility for their choices, accountability for the outcomes, and make no excuses for the situation.

The small business CEO described the challenging circumstances brought about by the pandemic and associated policy restrictions. She said that they would need to re-think all facets of the organization and how they would provide the service to their customers that had set them apart in the past. She encouraged them not to push back on the challenges but rather to embrace the opportunity as a means to grow beyond perceived limitations and to discover new capabilities. She concluded the discussion by suggesting that she had complete confidence in each of them and believed the solution to these challenges resided

95 Avey, J., Wernsing, M., & Palanski, M. (2012). Exploring the process of ethical leadership: The mediating role of employee voice and psychological ownership. *Journal of Business Ethics*, 107(1), 21–34.
96 Avey et al., 'Exploring the process of ethical leadership'.

in the skills and creativity of everyone in the room.

The concept of psychological ownership is a fascinating phenomenon in that the circumstances in which we assume ownership vary by individual. Yet, the ingredients that lead up to the events seem relatively consistent. You see, the same components that we have suggested build trust—transparent communications, establishing relational expectations, and enhancing personal and professional growth—all set the stage for empowering another to take ownership. Empowering another is the process of modeling, encouraging, and placing them in the position of assuming that they have a responsibility to make decisions in their own long-term best interest.

When the baby eagle or eaglet is born, it depends entirely on its parents for everything. As they grow, their parents model flight, encourage their growth by teaching them to spread their wings and hop from branch to branch, and eventually push them out of the nest to take that leap of faith and spread their wings to fly as a fledgling. The initial leap is unique to each bird, but the process leading up to that point is proven in nature. The same is true for humans.

I was the middle child of three siblings—the eldest boy in a family of five. My mother was a teacher and my father a chemist. As the eldest son, when my father would leave to go to work or on a business trip, he reminded me that I was the *man of the house* and had the responsibility to take care of my mother and siblings. It seemed like a privilege to me and little did I know that, at the age of nine, I *would* become the permanent *man of the house* when my father unexpectedly died in his sleep. He modeled the behavior, created the expectation, and prepared me for the unexpected leap of faith that would change not only my immediate life but also its future trajectory.

Just as that fledgling leaves the security and comfort of the nest with trepidation, once it has taken that step, the freedom and exhilaration associated with spreading its wings far outweigh its initial fear. So, it is clear: psychological ownership is counter-intuitive because the fears associated with responsibility and accountability are far outweighed by the freedom and exhilaration of spreading our wings. Pat Summitt, former Tennessee women's basketball coach and the most successful National Collegiate Athletic Association coach in history, suggested that *a sense of ownership* was the most powerful weapon a team or organization could have!

Coach Summitt understood the term "empowerment." It is not just about allowing your followers the opportunity to self-actualize and be all that they can be—it is also about unleashing the power behind their potential and allowing that power to free-flow into the organization or team. When followers are empowered to own their actions, account for the outcomes, and lead from their personal perspectives, it unleashes the power of potential, creating a catalyst for creativity and innovation.

When we look in the mirror, that is who we are. We own the reflection. The reflection houses our virtues, and our character is demonstrated by the consistency of our choices and actions. You see, the ownership we receive when we spread our wings not only reflects who we are but, more importantly, suggests who we have become. We become what we are empowered to be, which is directly related to our ownership displayed through commitment, effectiveness, and engagement.

Ownership Through Commitment

When a cadet graduates from the United States Air Force Academy, they incur a five-year active duty commitment and three years as an inactive reserve. Thus, the payback for a four-year undergraduate degree at one of the service academies is a commitment to serve in the military for a total of eight years. During these eight years, these individuals may be called upon to deploy to austere locations, give up their individual preferences for the good of the organization, and make the ultimate sacrifice by giving their life for their country. Before they accept their commission, in fact before their junior year, they acknowledge this commitment, freely accepting all consequences of the obligation in the knowledge that they are a part of something bigger than themselves.

Another well-known commitment revolves around the marriage vows when two people commit to have and to

193

hold, for better, for worse, for richer, for poorer, in sickness and in health, to love and to cherish, till death do they part. Like the graduation commitment, both parties publicly acknowledge the responsibility and accept the consequences of joining something bigger than themselves. Ironically, despite this relatively well-known and well-understood commitment, according to the American Psychological Association, the success rates for following through with this commitment are between 50% and 60%. This statistic suggests that committing and following through on those commitments may be two different things.

Interestingly, there are legal ramifications for breaking commitments that provide deterrents, yet people will endure these ramifications or look for ways around them. On the other hand, many people remain in a commitment without genuinely being committed to it, just to avoid the consequences of breaking it. But what about those who internalize the commitment? Seeing it as a part of themselves, who they are as a person, their character—if you will? Internalizing or ownership through commitment entails accepting responsibilities for choices, being mutually accountable for results, and remaining loyal to the cause or the *why*.

I was inspired by the advice pointing out that the most important job I could have is the one I have right now. Another great quote by Jim Rohn is, "Wherever you are, be there." He describes this as mastering the art of being. In simple terms, it is focusing on the present realizing that yesterday is gone and tomorrow hasn't arrived. Accept responsibility for today and the choices you make. While today's choices cannot change what has already occurred, they can influence future opportunities.

When life gets hard, and inevitably at times it does, accepting responsibility for the choices we have made is the first step to internalizing the commitments we have made, owning the circumstances, and eventually realizing the empowerment to navigate through life's challenges. I have often thought that each of us has a unique obstacle course designed for our lives such that, if we negotiate every obstacle placed in front of us, we will realize our purpose on this earth and experience life's greatest joy. Because we have free will, the choice is ours as to how we view life's obstacles and accept responsibility for the decisions we make.

When the eaglet is pushed from the nest, it has two choices: looking back to see what has happened or looking forward, spreading its wings and soaring. Often in life, what has happened has happened, and looking back does nothing for the way ahead. Taking responsibility for the present empowers us to determine the path ahead, experience the obstacles we face, and grow from the ownership of them. This growth occurs when we take the second step to ownership through commitment, being mutually accountable for the results.

We have spent a great deal of time talking about daring to be different and creating a culture of mutual accountability. We argued about whether finding joy in leadership is directly related to creating such a culture. Leaders who experience the joy of leadership understand the importance of their followers being mutually accountable for their results. When followers know that the consequences of their choices have an impact on the entire organization and remain intimately aware of the effects of those actions on one another, they are well on their way to demonstrating ownership through commitment.

If there was one common theme that resonated throughout the COVID-19 pandemic, being aware of the effects of our actions on one another was key to battling the virus and ensuring that we could operate within our communities and organizations. Perhaps there is no better story than the four Denver Bronco quarterbacks who decided to violate the league and team's COVID-19 protocols. By getting together for some *extra* work in the training facility when no one else was around, they violated several protocols to include the basic social distancing and mask-wearing requirements. Ironically, they intended to help the team prepare for their upcoming game against the New Orleans Saints by getting in some extra practice. Still, they did not consider the impact of potentially spreading the virus within the group and ended up risking the health of the entire team.

All the four Bronco quarterbacks were unable to compete in the game against the Saints because one of them tested positive and the other three had been exposed. The Broncos ended up using a running back for the team's quarterback and were handily defeated, 31–3, due to the lack of mutual accountability of these four professional athletes. Whether we agree or disagree with the policies and protocols we are faced with, we must take others into account. For example, there has been a lot of talk about the effectiveness of wearing a mask in dealing with the virus. While it may be true that most masks will not prevent the virus from penetrating the fabric, they do enhance our awareness of others and demonstrate courtesy and consideration for those around us.

COVID-19 demonstrated that individual choices can have societal consequences. Having an intimate awareness of the effects of our actions on others suggests a commitment to accountability beyond ourselves, and further reflects ownership and trust in our relationships with those around us. In COVID-19 terms, we must work together, despite our personal preferences and beliefs, for the good of society or the organization. Thus, the final step to ownership through commitment is demonstrating loyalty to the cause—in other words, internalizing *why* you are a part of the organization and *why* that organization exists.

In the special operations community, teams are compiled of individuals with unique capabilities to achieve an objective that no individual in the team could achieve independently. Only through the team's efforts and members' commitment to each other can the objective be accomplished. Each member must completely trust the others to do their jobs and to place the team above any personal desires. The common phrase, "there is no I in team," is not quaint: it is the difference between life and death.

The massive military cargo aircraft departed the west coast shortly after midnight to begin the 14-hour, 5,000-mile rescue flight in the South Pacific. A small 50-foot sailboat with a crew of two had sent out a distress signal to the rescue center in Hawaii, indicating that the boat's captain had become deathly ill due to an asthmatic reaction. Because the small sailboat's location (between Tahiti and Peru) was beyond the normal rescue aircrafts' range, this mission would require an aircraft capable of air refueling approximately five hours after departure to allow for five hours of search time to look for the tiny boat in the Pacific.

Takeaway: When followers clearly understand the objective—or the *why*—this elicits the relational self and personal identification with the leader, thereby enhancing the follower's own self-efficacy, self-esteem, and meaningfulness as well as their co-operation, loyalty and commitment to the leader.[97] In other words, when

---

97 Epitropaki, O., Kark, R., Mainemelis, C., & Lord, R. G. (2017). Leadership and followership identity processes: A multilevel review. *The Leadership Quarterly*, 28(1), 104–129. doi:10.1016/j.leaqua.2016.10.003

the purpose or objective is clear, followers demonstrate loyalty to the team, leader, and cause, placing all three above themselves and generating a positive sense of meaningfulness from their commitment. It is this phenomenon that explains why teams are willing to go above and beyond the call of duty to accomplish the objective.

The leaders of this rescue mission planned to start the search early in the morning so as to have the sun behind them. Based on the boat's last position, as well as the updates it was providing via high-frequency radio transmissions, the plane would descend to 4,000 feet and begin the search pattern looking for the proverbial needle in the haystack. If the team could locate the sailboat before returning within the maximum of five hours available for the search due to the fuel constraints, the plane would descend to 400 feet above the ocean and the crew would airdrop medication to the boat. But, once the aircraft had slowed down to descend to 400 feet for the airdrop, if the flaps (which are required to slow down a plane for an airdrop) did not come back up, the aircraft would have to ditch in the ocean, putting the lives of all 21 crew members at risk.

How much is a life worth? In this case, millions of dollars and 21 lives were committed to saving this small boat and its occupants. What is impressive about ownership through commitment is the responsibility, accountability, and loyalty it generates to motivate and empower both followers and leaders to go above and beyond the call of duty, as we see from this rescue mission example.

When that *why* is understood, and followers feel as though they belong to something bigger than themselves, biologically, their bodies release oxytocin, which has the power to regulate our emotional responses and pro-social behaviors, including trust, empathy, fond memories, and positive communication. Like the bond between a newborn and its mother, this trust goes to the very core, realizing the responsibility, accountability, and loyalty inherent in the bond commitment. Unfortunately, commitment alone cannot guarantee success in all life's challenges and this leads to the next evolution in who we become when we experience ownership and trust in a mutually accountable relationship: effective ownership.

Questions to consider:

- What is the relationship between commitment and trust within a leader–follower relationship?

- How can previously made commitments change over time?

Effective Ownership

Experiencing ownership and trust through commitment empowers us through responsibility, accountability, and loyalty to the organization, team, and relationship. But what happens after we have been empowered with that ownership? One of the greatest, and perhaps timeless, illustrations of empowered ownership is Matthew 25: 14–30, *The Parable of Talents*.[98]

This parable tells of a master who was leaving his house to travel and, before leaving, entrusted his property to three of his servants. According to their abilities, each received talents (a measure of gold). The first received five, the second two, and the third only one. When their master left, the servants, empowered by their talents, decided how to use them while their master was gone. On his return, he met with the servants to hear how they had used their talents.

The servant who was given five talents turned his five into ten. His master was delighted and replied, "Well done, good and faithful servant. You have been faithful over a little; I will set you over much. Enter the joy of your master." The servant who received two doubled his talents and ended up with four. His master was delighted as well and replied the same. The servant who received one talent had dug a hole and buried it when his master left; therefore, he presented him with the one talent upon his return. His master replied, "You wicked and slothful servant, you have done nothing with what I had given you," and he took the talent away and gave it to the one who had received five.

---

98 Bible, New International Version, 2016, (Matthew 25:14–30).

As this parable points out, effective ownership is not passive but instead an active and ever-evolving engagement. We have already established that leaders who model ethical practices bring out the best in their employees through psychological empowerment that facilitates their current success and success potential. The same 2018 study found that leaders who model ethical practices inspire their followers to think critically for themselves, take ownership of their decisions, and make complex decisions independently.[99] It is very clear: effective ownership requires initiative, creativity, and ingenuity.

The COVID-19 pandemic hit the aviation industry extremely hard. Before the pandemic, the industry was at record highs with expected growth throughout. For young aviators entering the industry, the opportunity for 30+ year careers never seemed better. Then the realization of COVID-19 lock-downs hit the industry as abruptly and severely as the post-9/11 fallout. With thousands of airplanes being sent to the desert during the uncertainty of the times, what was once a robust industry was now hanging by a thread.

While the legacy airlines (American, Delta, and United) and many of the larger major airlines were lobbying Congress for financial support as they had done post-9/11 with bailout funding, a small privately owned, ultra-low-cost airline decided it would seize the initiative during this time of crisis with a focus on thriving

---

99 Dust et al., 'Ethical leadership and employee success'.

versus surviving. The Frontier Airlines CEO decided to require all passengers and crew members to wear a mask and have their temperature taken. This initiative was implemented well ahead of all other airlines and eventually government guidance on mask requirements. Additionally, Frontier was among the first in the industry to explain the HEPA filters' effectiveness in capturing 99.9% of airborne particles.

By seizing the initiative, Frontier decided to own the situation and do everything it could to protect the passengers who chose to travel. Also, during this time of recovery, the airline re-imagined what thriving on the other side of the pandemic would look like. It established a goal to be the greenest airline fleet in the industry, striving to be "America's Greenest Airline." Like the example provided earlier with Chick-fil-A seizing the initiative by restructuring their drive-thru to give a better experience for their customers, Frontier was doing the same for the airline industry.

When followers have been empowered by leaders they trust, they internalize their commitment to the organization and relationship by taking the initiative to advance the cause designed to realize the objective—the *why*, or the reason for existence within the organization. Because Steve Jobs made the Apple vision of putting a personal computer in the hands of every human being so clear, every Apple employee and enthusiast feels empowered to encourage that vision to become a reality. I was actually the last person in my family to switch to the

MAC and not because I was unhappy with my previous PCs. I changed because everyone in my family convinced me that it was the best choice (and they didn't even get a commission!).

Besides seizing the initiative to make ownership more active and effective, when followers are empowered and trust the leadership and the organization, they unleash creativity toward problem-solving and advancing the organization and its reason for being. Remember the story of the Service Disabled Small Business team that decided to bid for work in the National Capital Region that a billion-dollar aerospace company had previously performed? By unleashing its creativity, the team came up with a winning proposal and earned their customers' and competitors' respect and admiration.

Workplace competition has not become more manageable with the changes brought about by the COVID-19 pandemic. If anything, it has become more complex and challenging, requiring more creativity and ingenuity. It may take years to realize the impact of fewer face-to-face conversations and employees' interactions within an organization. But those like Frontier Airlines that wish to thrive will need to encourage and capture employee creativity to advance the organization's long-term survival. Unfortunately, cultural engagement trends discourage any creative thinking that dissents from the views of the leader or the majority of the organization. Those organizations that wish to thrive in this new competitive environment will need leaders that encourage creative thinking.

As the large cargo aircraft began its descent to 4,000 feet above the Pacific Ocean, it contacted the small 50-foot sailboat. The Captain's wife was literally piloting the boat, taking care of her dying husband, and communicating with the aircraft. She provided her current latitude and longitude based on her on-board satellite navigation system. Although this would appear to pinpoint her position, a 50-foot sailboat in the middle of the Pacific could easily be missed among the whitecaps and vast ocean.

During the communications with the aircraft, the Captain's wife asked if she should have her sail up or keep it down and remain fixed in her last known position. When the aircraft commander was queried on this question, he replied, "Let's have her keep it down, and we will make our way to her last known position." Immediately, the navigator—an avid sailor—suggested that, without the sail up, the small boat would be nearly impossible to identify. This creative spot-on suggestion would prove to be paramount to this rescue mission's success.

When leaders create a mutually accountable culture based on trust within the organization or team, members feel free to offer creative solutions that may be in direct conflict with the leader's current guidance or direction. Research suggests that leaders should provide their followers with useful information and encourage them to voice their new or different ideas while fostering a trust that dispels any fear of creativity failures.[100] In other words, there are no bad creative ideas and followers need to trust that.

Because the aircraft commander had fostered a trusting environment within the 21-person crew and each member felt ownership of the rescue mission, the idea to keep the sail up won through and a small boat was spotted within 20 minutes of beginning the search! Leaders need to understand that they never know where the solutions to their challenges may come from, so they must foster an environment encouraging all members to think creatively without fear of failure to develop a solution.

Takeaway: When leaders inspire initiative and creativity to enhance ownership effectiveness, they open the doors to encouraging ingenuity, the third component to effective ownership. Whereas creativity is about creating an environment in which followers are free to think unconventionally to allow the creative juices to flow, ingenuity is about taking empowerment

---

100 Qu et al., 'Leader–member exchange'.

to the next level and applying that creativity to resolving the challenge or problem at hand. The deep investment leaders make by creating mutually accountable cultures effectively multiplies as their followers act as managerial proxies in training and mentoring other group members to do the same.[101]

It goes without saying that leaders are problem solvers, but the joy in leadership is not about the number of problems solved. Finding joy in leadership is about developing your followers to seize the initiative, employ their creativity, come up with ingenious solutions on their own, and—ultimately—advise you of a solution, if not a problem solved. By encouraging transparent communications, establishing relational expectations, enhancing personal and professional growth, and experiencing ownership through commitment and effectiveness, trust within the mutually accountable relationship grows, and the bond of purpose and belonging is reinforced.

Biologically, our bodies release oxytocin and the bond between leader and follower grows, perpetuating the cycle of communication, expectation, growth, and ownership, and further increasing the biological bond and established trust. This experience transforms the follower and the leader as each grows in ownership and trust within this mutually accountable relationship. This leads us to the final factor in experiencing ownership and

---

101 Herdman, A., Yang, J., & Arthur, J. (2017). How does leader-member exchange disparity affect teamwork behavior and effectiveness in work groups? The moderating role of leader-leader exchange. *Journal of Management*, 43(5), 1549–1523.

trust while realizing who we are becoming: ownership engagement.

Questions to consider:

- Why is effective ownership considered a "force multiplier" for leaders?

- How have leaders in your past empowered you toward further ownership within the organization, and how did that make you feel about those leaders?

Ownership Engagement

In a 2018 systematic literature review of employee engagement and performance, the author stated, "low-level employee engagement at work is currently one of the most alarming global economic problems at work".[102] We would expect declining work performance to follow if employees are not engaged in their work. Also, if this was the trend in 2018 when employees were physically present in the workplace, what would it look like in the pandemic, stay-at-home, virtual workplace that currently affects so many around the globe?

I worked for a small business owner who suggested that the difference between an employee and an owner is the difference between a chicken and a pig. For the chicken to provide an egg, it has to complete the expected process of laying an egg. For the pig to provide the bacon, it has to give its life. While this may sound

102 Motyka, B. (2018). Employee engagement and performance: A systematic literature review. *Academy of Management Review*, 54(3), 227–244.

like an extreme example of ownership, the reality is that, when we *own* something, quite often we need to be fully committed! We have described this as a commitment based on responsibility, accountability, and loyalty.

When they signed on to Shackleton's Antarctic exploration, there is no doubt that the crew members were all fully committed first to the exploration and then to survival. Their survival's effectiveness was augmented by their initiative, creativity, and ultimately ingenuity. Every member was actively engaged in the day-to-day tasks from start to finish. This engagement was defined by their relationships, trust within those relationships, and their dependence on one another.

Custom Insight is a company specializing in tools to help companies engage and develop their employees, managers, and leaders more effectively. They define employee engagement as "the extent to which employees feel passionate about their jobs, are committed to the organization, and put discretionary effort into their work."[103] To realize this level of engagement requires trust in the relationships concerned. These are the mutually accountable relationships in which each person is constantly aware of the impact of their actions on the other and holding each other accountable.

The phone rang at 2 a.m. startling the Air Force officer out of a deep sleep. She cleared her voice

---

103 Custominsight.com (n.d.) What is employee engagement? https://www.custominsight.com/employee-engagement-survey/what-is-employee-engagement.asp

a couple of times before answering the phone. On the other end was her commander, a man she implicitly trusted and for whom she had the utmost respect. "We have a mission I need you to lead that departs in four hours. I can't tell you where it is going right now or how long you will be gone, but I can tell you that it is of utmost importance and you are the right person to lead this effort." The officer replied, "Yes, sir, understood. Tell me when and where to report."

When the leader–follower relationship is mutually accountable, followers will often commit to making a special effort for their leaders, engaging as if the relationship depended on their effort. Or, put differently, when followers engage, based on their relationship with their leader and the organization, their *why* is crystal clear and meaningful to who they are and why they are engaged.

Patrick Mahomes, 2020 Superbowl Most Valuable Player (MVP), describes his leader Coach Andy Reid this way: "Coach Reid is a great teacher. He understands how people learn, understands how to get people to get the concept of what the play is and why we are running it." Followers actively engage in relationships when both parties understand *why* each is engaged and *why* that engagement is vital to the organization. We engage with those we can relate to. Thus, it is incumbent on a leader to ensure that their followers understand *why* they are asked to do what they do and *why* that is important to the organization. This understanding leads them to the next key factor for ownership engagement: trust.

When the Air Force officer accepted the *unknown* mission from her leader, she did so based not only on the mutually accountable relationship with her boss but also because she trusted that he had her best interests in mind and believed she would be successful. Leaders committed to developing ownership in their followers understand that trust allows their followers to fully invest in the tasks required to reach their goals, absent of any fear of the leader taking advantage of or mistreating them.[104]

I have researched and authored various articles over the past few years in my endeavor to gain a greater understanding of mutually accountable relationships in the workplace. At this point, I believe that, more than any other issue assessed through this process, the one to stand out is trust. Repeatedly, participants identified trust as an important element in accountability based on efficiency, harmony, and influence.[105] Without trust, it is hard to believe that we can establish mutually accountable relationships. As mentioned previously, during the COVID-19 pandemic, the inconsistencies

104 Nichols, A., & Cottrell, C. (2014). What do people desire in their leaders? The role of leadership level on trait desirability. *The Leadership Quarterly*, 25(4), 711–729.
105 Phillips, R. (2020). *The Perception of Mutual Accountability within the LMX: Its Influence on the Supervisor and Employee Relationship*. A dissertation presented in partial fulfillment of the requirements for the degree Doctorate of Philosophy, Grand Canyon University, Phoenix, Arizona.

in guidance and behaviors from leaders throughout the United States made it hard to trust those prescribing the best way to deal with the crisis.

The inconsistencies in guidance led to inconsistencies in engagement with that guidance. Consistency is critical to developing trust within an organization. Leaders who wish to build ownership in followers through engagement must realize that any inconsistencies in their behavior can destroy trust in seconds. This point reinforces all the previously discussed process steps: transparent communications, relational expectations, and personal and professional growth are continually feeding ownership within an organization. In other words, none of these steps is adequate in itself in developing trust through mutually accountable relationships. Instead, each is vital to and dependent on the others, which leads to the last component of ownership engagement: dependence.

Takeaway: When leaders empower their followers and each can relate to the other within an environment of trust, followers remain engaged, acknowledging their leader's dependence on their ownership and their own reliance on support from their leader. Human beings are social creatures. We are designed to interact with others, and yet, in many cases, we are often ill-equipped for these interactions. This strange dependence creates a unique opportunity for those who can break the *equipping* code. As we finish up the discussion of "Experiencing Ownership and Trust: *Who* We Become," it is only fitting that we finish with a discussion of dependence.

Dealing with human beings is a dynamic and never-ending challenge. As we continue to evolve and grow in our understanding, augmented by new technologies and theories, it is no surprise that every generation is quite different and focused on priorities unique to that cohort. Psychologists continue to learn more about human behavior and still have yet to fully explain why we do the things we do. As was suggested at the beginning of this book, there are over 57,000 Amazon books with leadership in the title, so we might conclude that leadership remains a curious phenomenon.

Within each of these areas—human behavior, psychology, and leadership—lie four common denominators: communications, relations, growth, and ownership. Engaging followers within the workplace requires leaders to depend on their abilities to address all four. By effectively creating a culture of mutual accountability with their followers, leaders empower them to grow within the organization through their commitment, effectiveness, and engagement. In doing so, leaders demonstrate their dependence on their followers, and their followers acknowledge their reliance on the culture.

What makes leadership, psychology, and understanding human behavior so frustrating is our misguided belief that all these areas have been precisely defined. We design policies and procedures around the past instead of understanding the present to better predict the future. Wayne Gretzky, the *Greatest of All Time* hockey player we introduced in Part III, would describe this as dealing with leadership where it is, instead of dealing with it where it is going to be. We can never understand who each of us can become if we don't first accept each other for who they are. To remain engaged as leaders and followers, we must depend on a process we can trust, and one that has proven to build trust: creating a culture of mutual accountability by encouraging transparent communications, establishing relational expectations, enhancing personal and professional growth, and experiencing ownership.

When leaders and followers understand *why* trust matters, *how* trust has an impact on an organization, *what* trust does for a relationship, and *who* they can become in a mutually accountable relationship, they realize the importance of developing trust you can count on. By daring to be different and creating a culture of mutual accountability, leaders can employ this proven process and find joy in leadership.

Questions to consider:

- What is the greatest organizational benefit to having employees actively engaged in the workplace?

- Why are some leaders threatened by empowering their followers and—perhaps—eventually working themselves out of a job?

Part VI Recap:
Developing Trust You Can Count On:
The What and The Who

Enhancing Personal/Professional Growth: What Trust Does for a Relationship

- When trust exists within a relationship, followers feel the security and affirmation needed to think unconventionally and *find creative and ingenious solutions*.
- Leaders have the opportunity to *model and develop character*, and thus influence those within their spheres to do the same.
- When trust exists between leaders and followers in a mutually accountable relationship, leaders feel free to challenge and encourage their followers to *realize their potential*, and their followers are willing to take the risk to realize that potential.

Experiencing Ownership and Trust: Who We Become

- When the purpose or objective is clear, followers demonstrate loyalty and remain committed to the team, leader, and cause, seeing the cause as more important than themselves and realizing a positive sense of meaningfulness in doing so.
- Leaders who model ethical practices inspire their followers to think critically for themselves, take ownership of their decisions, and make complex decisions independently. In other words, *effective* ownership requires initiative, creativity, and ingenuity.
- When a leader empowers their follower, and each can relate to the other within an environment of trust, the follower remains engaged, acknowledging their leader's dependence on their ownership and the follower's reliance on support from their leader.

Part VII:

Finding the Joy

L et's face it: leadership is hard work! No matter how you craft it, there is no easy path to effective leadership. A good friend of mine likened leadership to climbing 14,000-foot peaks ("14ers") in Colorado. No matter how you try and spin it, there are no easy 14ers. Although each starts somewhat predictably, their unique personality and challenges, combined with Mother Nature's surprises and physiological constraints, create anything but a routine climb to the top. What makes the journey more enjoyable is sharing it with others, ensuring proper preparation, taking in the view along the way, and appreciating the gift of the opportunity to take on the climb.

It seems absurd that anyone would take to climbing a 14er on their own, rushing to get to the top, reaching the top, patting themselves on the back, then looking for another 14er to climb, and doing the same. But, as absurd as this may sound, too many leaders are focused on building their resumes and making money without ever "taking in the view along the way". Their goal is to survive the leadership experience just long enough to gain the reward of a higher-level position. Thomas Merton describes this as "climbing the ladder of success only to find, once they reach the top, that the ladder is leaning against the wrong wall".[106]

We started this discussion in Part I by looking at the difference between reward and joy. As you will recall, rewards are short-lived feelings based on the release of dopamine after a promotion, accolade, gift, or other pleasant event. These rewards are ours alone and rarely involve association with others. Conversely, joy is found in creating a bond with another human being based on the development of trust within the relationship. The interaction itself is where we find joy, well-being, and happiness due to the biological release of dopamine and serotonin.

As bonds strengthen and relationships grow, our bodies release oxytocin that supports social recognition, trust, and respect. Like climbing a 14er, effective leadership requires adequate preparation, taking in the view along the way and sharing the pleasure of it with those around us. Leaders need to clearly understand why they chose a leadership position, and the inherent challenges and dangers they face. Leadership is hard work, so how we perceive our role and interaction with those we are privileged to lead will determine our ability to find joy on the journey.

Human beings are complex creatures. From our first breath to our last, we continually analyze our place on this earth in an attempt to understand our purpose and how we fit in. As we described in Part III, we navigate

---

106 Thomas Merton quotes—Azquotes. https://www.azquotes.com/quote/856466

our unique circumstances throughout life to satisfy our basic affirmation and security needs, which sometimes compete with our inherent selfish nature. The tension between nurturing and understanding ourselves causes the dilemma between reward and joy.

This tension is why investing in creating a culture of mutual accountability is initially more complicated than just *holding followers accountable*. Mutual accountability requires both parties to think about others as much as, or more than, themselves. The most significant benefit of this investment in daring to be different is the opportunity to develop a bond of trust that encourages transparent communications, establishes relational expectations, enhances personal and professional growth, and empowers ownership.

When trust is the foundation of the leader–follower relationship, followers feel affirmed for who they are and secure in taking the initiative, expressing their creativity, and exercising their ingenuity. Finding joy in leadership is directly related to this transformation as the leader realizes the fruits of their investment in the follower's greater commitment, effectiveness, and engagement. Due to their commitment to modeling the virtues they wish to see in their followers, leaders can view the benefits of their labor in the eyes and actions of those they have the privilege of leading. Thus, joy is found in the relationships, the workplace, and even cultural settings—wherever the bond of trust has been established.

Finding Joy in Relationships

The 60-year-old retired high school science teacher stepped out of his car and entered the grocery store to pick up a few items for the weekend. It had been over 10 years since his retirement, and he was enjoying the slower pace of his men's golf group and spending time with his wife and grandchildren. As he was waiting at the checkout, a woman addressed him by name as she approached him and said she was so happy to see him. She described the impact he had made on her life and how his example had encouraged her to go on and also teach high school science. He had not seen her in over 10 years, but he remembered that she was one of seven children who had all worked at the family-owned bakery in town.

When leaders take the time to relate to their followers through transparent communications, relational expectations, personal and professional growth, and ownership, they create relationships and bonds with those followers that may last a lifetime. Mutually accountable relationships assume an intimate awareness of the impact of our actions on another, with each holding the other accountable for progress and outcomes. Creating mutually accountable relationships is about considering others as more important than ourselves and willingly investing in them to realize their potential.

The retired teacher exited the checkout and entered the car on the driver's side. Before putting the keys in the ignition, he paused and smiled, thinking to himself that you never know the impact you may make on those within your sphere of influence. He thought, "Perhaps I *have* made a difference." Joy filled his heart!

Research affirms that, when leaders ensure that their followers can relate to their leadership in a high-quality way, their followers are more satisfied at work and experience greater career success.[107]

This greater success implies that, in addition to a leader experiencing joy as they realize their impact on their followers, a follower experiences joy as they discover their potential. This joy-filled relationship, based on implicit trust, allows the leader to encourage their followers to try to achieve a challenge—and to believe that they can. Remember the story about Anthony Robles, the Division I wrestling champion? His college coach believed that he could achieve the peak in his wrestling pursuits. He never said it would be easy, but instead invested in a relationship that would build a powerful bond of success and thereby

107 Hsiung, H., & Bolino, M. (2018). The implications of perceived leader favouritism in the context of leader-member exchange relationships. *European Journal of Work and Organizational Psychology*, 27(1), 88–99. doi:10.1080/1359432X.2017.1395414

bring joy to them both. This was also a superb example of an effective mutually accountable relationship.

Finding the joy in relationships described by these two examples may be more difficult in the new world created by the COVID-19 pandemic. Virtual meetings, classrooms, and reduced gatherings suggest it may be harder to build the bond of trust that leads to success and joy. What is clear from the impact of lockdowns, social distancing, and mask-wearing is that people feel more isolated, less connected, and lonelier than in decades past. Even before the pandemic, research suggests that the strength of relationships in virtual teams is considerably weaker than that found in face-to-face contexts.[108]

As leaders, we must be mindful of the impact of virtual operations in place of face-to-face engagements. The benefits of building strong bonds with those we lead may very well be what distinguishes good from great, because those who can tap into the creativity and ingenuity within their organizations are likely to outperform those who cannot.

Finding Joy in the Workplace

We spent Part III of this book addressing why leadership is not always enjoyable. The reality is that the journey and the climb to the top require consistent discipline and drive. Within the context of great athletes like Michael Jordan and Tiger Woods, we highlighted how achieving joy at the top involves constant growth and correction,

108 Charlier, S., Stewart, G., Greco, L., & Reeves, C. (2016). Emergent leadership in virtual teams: A multilevel investigation of individual communication and team dispersion antecedents. *Leadership Quarterly*, 27(5), 745–764.

delighting in feedback, and never losing sight of the goal. It is that *daring to be different* attitude—knowing that it may require the path less traveled but believing in the process and the discipline to stick to it.

Building a culture of mutual accountability is such a path less traveled and definitely requires the discipline to stick with it. Yet, this entire process addresses and mitigates each of the areas we described in Part III that typically rob a leader of the joy of leadership: dealing with the problems people face; adopting a positive attitude toward problem-solving; maintaining a far-sighted perspective; and keeping why we lead at the forefront. Let's look at each one.

Dealing with the problems people face requires one to understand the need for affirmation and security, and to acknowledge man's innate selfish desire. By investing in a mutually accountable relationship, leaders establish that bond of trust that allows followers to express themselves creatively and also empowers them to exercise their ingenuity. The predictability of the process minimizes speculation, thereby reducing the stress associated with unknowns in the workplace. Both leaders and followers act together as a team to realize the trust and freedom needed to address workplace issues and challenges in the best interests of the organization and their relationship.

This approach addresses the second principle that typically removes joy from the workplace: a negative attitude toward problem-solving. When leaders and followers embrace workplace concerns and challenges as opportunities for growth, they foster an environment of empowerment in which creativity and ingenuity proactively find solutions. Problems are no longer viewed as burdens to bear but rather opportunities to make the team and organization stronger and better equipped to serve their customers. This shift from problem to opportunity also shifts the focus from where we are to where we want to be, which addresses the third determinant of joy in the workplace: maintaining a far-sighted perspective.

The difference between surviving and thriving often lies within our focal point. When the *Endurance* was trapped in the ice and it became clear that the ship would eventually succumb to the pressure of the crushing ice, Shackleton shifted his focus from the South Pole to the safe return of all of his crew members. Had he just focused on surviving the day-to-day challenges of the Antarctic, there might not have been any survivors. Creating a mutually accountable culture is about trusting the best in yourself and those you lead, relying on the foundation of your processes, training, and experience. This outward focus addresses the final key to finding joy in the workplace: keeping the *why* one leads at the forefront.

By focusing outward, leaders keep their followers first in mind, which is aligned with the *why* for leading. They avoid the temptation of seeking affirmation from their supervisors at the cost of taking care of those they are entrusted to lead, and they open their minds toward discovering new skills, capabilities, and opportunities in and for their followers. This outward focus aligns with the mutual accountability process and models the selflessness this process requires.

When leaders keep their focus outward, they can assess the effectiveness of their communications, relational expectations, personal and professional growth in their followers, and their ownership within the organization. Just as a farmer keeps a watchful eye on their crops to protect them from the elements of the environment, leaders must ensure that the typical elements of the workplace do not erode the bonds of trust they have worked so hard to establish. By keeping a watchful eye and ensuring the best for their followers, they can realize the greatest joy associated with a mutually accountable culture.

The Joy of Cultural Impact: The Law of Sowing and Reaping

As discussed in Part V, the beauty of the law of sowing and reaping is how you almost always reap much more than you have sowed. You already know how I tasted the joy of leading and what it took to achieve it. My passion is for all leaders to experience joy and for their organizations to thrive under their leadership. I was privileged to serve selfless leaders who influenced me greatly in better understanding leadership and the joy inherent in it. It was never about their success—it was always about the privilege to lead.

I introduced you to a leader I worked for who was the most incredible listener I have ever met. He was also the most *transparent and effective communicator* I have ever known. We discussed the impact Sully Sullenberger had had on the lives of those in his airplane when he had to make the split-second decision to land in the Hudson. Because he had ensured that the entire crew knew his *expectations* and he knew theirs, his legacy will be about the "Miracle on the Hudson" and not the tens of thousands of hours he flew as a commercial pilot.

We learned about the extraordinary *personal and professional growth* of Anthony Robles—the fact that a one-legged wrestler could make it to the top of the intercollegiate ladder because he had coaches who encouraged and believed in him. This story illustrates the impact that leaders can have when unleashing their creativity and potential in a trusting, mutually accountable relationship.

Finally, this book has been about you! You would not have reached this page unless you had wanted to experience the joy of leadership by having a positive impact on those you have the privilege of leading. Like many leaders before you, you may have fallen into the trap of day-to-day survival, or you may have lost your purpose in leading or the joy of leadership. You may remember that feeling of wanting to have an impact on your followers the same way that some exceptional leaders had influenced and inspired *you*!

Unfortunately, along the way, your focus has shifted from thriving to surviving. You need a roadmap to get you back on the path to thriving and to keep you on the path to experiencing the joy of leadership. That is why I have written this book. Developing a mutually accountable culture is a proven way to create trust you can count on, thereby releasing joy for leaders and followers alike. Leadership is hard—and there is no way around this. But the joy of leadership is attainable: dare to be different and create a culture of mutual accountability whereby leaders and followers alike will feel the affirmation, security, and trust they desire—consciously or unconsciously...

In the Introduction to this book, I promised to give you the following:

- A proven approach to building trust in leadership relationships.

- A common-sense approach to effective leadership.

- A formula for relishing the leadership experience and so making the workplace enjoyable for both leaders and followers.

- A procedure for bridging the gap between the MBA curriculum and practical leadership.

- A "predictability" within the leadership relationship to reduce the stress of speculation and expectation.

- A positive "team" atmosphere whereby all team members know *why* they are there and *how* their actions support that purpose.

- A process that can be applied to any leadership theory and style.

This proven, common-sense approach to bridging the gap between management theory and leadership practice is based on the principle of committing to an intimate awareness of the effects of our actions on another, and holding each other accountable for progress and outcomes. The commitment to dare to be different and create a culture of mutual accountability by encouraging transparent communications, establishing relational expectations, enhancing personal and professional growth, and experiencing ownership establishes a bond of trust within a relationship that can last a lifetime.

This bond of trust enhances any leadership theory and style, and the process that builds the trust provides predictability that minimizes anxieties of speculation and expectation. Finally, the process is perpetual in that the cycle never stops. As followers experience ownership within a relationship, new questions arise that require a transparent discussion of expectations and opportunities. These perpetuate the ongoing cycle of enhanced trust, shared growth, and invested ownership. Within this cycle, our purpose becomes more apparent and the joy of the journey becomes the reward.

Dare to be Different and Find Joy in Leadership!

Index